THE **ALL NEW** ILLUSTRATED GUIDE
TO **EVERYTHING SOLD** IN
HARDWARE ST**O**RES

SARAH & RYAN,

OLD HOUSES ARE GEMS!

YOU MIGHT NEED A LOT

OF THIS STUFF FOR YOURS ☺

I'D LOVE TO INSTALL IT FOR YOU.

I LOVE YOU,

Scott

XMAS 2020

Brimming with creative inspiration, how-to projects, and useful information to enrich your everyday life, Quarto Knows is a favorite destination for those pursuing their interests and passions. Visit our site and dig deeper with our books into your area of interest: Quarto Creates, Quarto Cooks, Quarto Homes, Quarto Lives, Quarto Drives, Quarto Explores, Quarto Gifts, or Quarto Kids.

© 2017 Quarto Publishing Group USA Inc.
First-edition text © 2003 Running Press

First Published in 2017 by Cool Springs Press, an imprint of The Quarto Group, 100 Cummings Center, Suite 265-D, Beverly, MA 01915, USA. T (978) 282-9590 F (978) 283-2742
QuartoKnows.com

Cool Springs Press titles are also available at discount for retail, wholesale, promotional, and bulk purchase. For details, contact the Special Sales Manager by email at specialsales@quarto.com or by mail at The Quarto Group, Attn: Special Sales Manager, 100 Cummings Center, Suite 265-D, Beverly, MA 01915, USA.

10 9 8 7 6 5 4

ISBN: 978-1-59186-686-2

Library of Congress Cataloging-in-Publication Data

Names: Ettlinger, Steve, author. | Schmidt, Philip, author.
Title: The all new illustrated guide to everything sold in hardware stores /
    Steve Ettlinger & Phil Schmidt.
Other titles: Complete illustrated guide to everything sold in hardware stores
Description: Minneapolis, MN : Quarto Publishing Group USA, Inc., [2017]
Identifiers: LCCN 2016052148 | ISBN 9781591866862 (sc)
Subjects: LCSH: Hardware--United States--Catalogs. | Hardware--Terminology.
Classification: LCC TS405 .E79 2017 | DDC 683--dc23
LC record available at https://lccn.loc.gov/2016052148

Acquiring Editor: Bryan Trandem
Project Manager: Alyssa Bluhm
Art Director: James Kegley
Cover Designer: Kim Winscher
Layout: Kim Winscher
Photography: Lightbox Images

PHOTO CREDITS
Shutterstock: 5, 6, 9, 67, 99, 129, 147, 197

Printed in China

THE **ALL NEW** ILLUSTRATED GUIDE TO **EVERYTHING SOLD** IN HARDWARE STRES

BY STEVE ETTLINGER & PHILIP SCHMIDT

COOL
SPRINGS
PRESS

This book is dedicated to all of us who have ever walked into a hardware store, home center, or lumberyard and asked for a *whatchamacallit* or *thingamajig*.

PREFACE

This is the latest iteration of a book that first hit the shelves back in 1988, and which has seen a few updates and many, many readers over the years. Its uncommon longevity and popularity can be attributed to two things. First, it's a great concept: a book that helps you identify what you need *before* you get to the hardware store and start scanning its endless merchandise. And second, it's a universally helpful resource: who *doesn't* need help with hardware? Most folks feel lost in hardware stores, and even tradespeople and handy homeowners have gray areas. You may be able to singlehandedly build a shed or retile a bathroom, but do you know the difference between an AFCI and a GFCI? (This book tells you, by the way.)

If you're out shopping for an electrical outlet, you actually do need to know the difference between an AFCI and a GFCI. Just like you need to know when stainless-steel screws are worth the cost and why not to use duct tape on ducts. These kinds of details were the inspiration for the original version of this book, and are the reasons for this new edition. While some things haven't changed much over the last few decades—houses are still built largely with nails, and deck stain still needs to be reapplied more often than we'd like—hardware products are constantly changing, as are the rules for using them properly and safely in your house. The updated content and new, color photos in this edition will help you find just what you need for today's projects.

Perhaps what's changed most of all is the hardware store itself. Hardware retailers have always carried a wide variety of items—it's the nature of the business—but today's large home centers have taken selection to a whole new level, some offering upwards of 40,000 different products under one roof. They're well staffed, for sure, but it still helps enormously to have a good idea of what you need when you get in the door. After all, out of those 40,000 items, you might be in search of exactly one. And that's why this book is more necessary and, we hope, more helpful than ever.

—*Phil Schmidt*, Edition Editor

CONTENTS

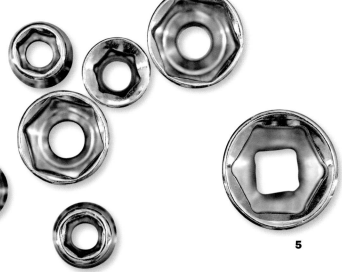

INTRODUCTION

WHY THIS BOOK

Whether you are a homeowner, an apartment dweller, or a renovator, you no doubt have often entered a hardware store, lumberyard, or home center full of fear prior to making a small purchase.

Probably the most frustrating thing is that when you ask a clerk for an item—whether a succinct request for a paintbrush or pliers, or the more typical "whatchamacallit that fits over the thing that you turn to make the doohickey work" (accompanied, no doubt, by broad, dramatic, descriptive hand gestures)—the clerk will come back at you, nine times out of ten, with a barrage of questions: "Well, what are you using it for?" "What size do you want?" "You want top-of-the-line or cheap?" "Silicone or acrylic?" "Galvanized or plain?" If you haven't thought these questions through, this can be pretty demoralizing, embarrassing, and intimidating. I know. That's just the kind of experience that gave birth to this book.

The All New Illustrated Guide to Everything Sold in Hardware Stores should serve to end your intimidation, help you avoid wrong purchases, and enable even you, too, to walk fearlessly into a hardware store or lumberyard and get exactly what you need.

HOW THIS BOOK IS ORGANIZED

The more common items are in the front of each section, and groups of items follow this in a logical sequence wherever possible.

The item names are the result of months of research with manufacturers and catalogs, and though the names reflect the most accurate and common terms you'll find on a store's label, in many cases it may not be the name with which you are most familiar—the name you hear on the job site, for example. That's where the "Also Known As" element for each item comes into play. The idea for this section comes from the original inspiration for this book, when someone told me to get a cat's paw, which is not the most common name for the tool I needed, more properly called a nail claw.

We all call these tools by the names we've learned informally—from where we grew up, in the Navy, on the farm, from some old boss who picked up hardware nomenclature from who knows where. It has been fun collecting all the various aliases that might be out there. Some are dead wrong and may come from authoritative sources (even a popular TV show host), others are rare and folkloric. But someone, somewhere, calls the thing by that name, and so it finds its way into print.

"About" sections cover the basics of broad categories, such as screws or electrical switches.

"Description" tells you what the item looks like and notes key features, and "Use" tells you what it's most commonly used for.

"Use Tips" expand on one or more uses for the items and offer expert advice on specific applications.

"Buying Tips" help you choose between more or less expensive options, suggest an essential purchase, or help you distinguish one type from another.

WHAT THIS BOOK DOES NOT INCLUDE

Though a good hardware store, lumberyard, or home center carries tens and even hundreds of thousands of items in stock, this book includes only those that the average homeowner/handyperson will find necessary for typical repairs and DIY projects. It does not include many items used primarily by professionals or things that are used most commonly in commercial buildings. And because selection varies so much regionally, we have excluded most tools from this volume.

There is also a conscious avoidance of extensive how-to advice. The tips given are meant to echo the friendly advice a good clerk would give you as you leave a store; they are definitely not the comprehensive and detailed instructions required for many projects.

—*Steve Ettlinger*, author

PART I
GENERAL HARDWARE

CHAPTER 1

NAILS

ABOUT NAILS

There are two categories of nails: those ordinarily used for assembling wood members, be it fine work or rough construction, and specialized nails—those having a variety of single purposes. Actually, there are hundreds of different types when you include various esoteric coatings, ends, materials, and heads. Here, we deal only with the more commonly found ones. Most of the regular nails for wood may be referred to as wire nails.

For wood, though you can get nails smaller and larger, nails are generally available in 1- to 6-inch sizes; as the nail gets longer it gets larger and thicker in diameter. After 6 inches in length, nails are often called spikes and can range up to 18 inches long.

Basic wood nails are sized according to length, expressed by the letter *d* (verbalized as "penny"). Originally this was an early English symbol for a pound of weight—from the ancient Roman coin, the denarius—and related to the weight of 1,000 nails in pounds. Some say it was the cost of 100 nails in pence, abbreviated "d." Sizes run from 2d (2-penny or 1 inch long) to 60d (60-penny or 6 inches long)—6d nails are 2 inches long, 10d nails are 3 inches long, etc. This is shown on the following table.

NAIL SIZING

2d—1"	5d—1¾"	8d—2½"	12d—3½"	30d—4½"	60d—6"
3d—1¼"	6d—2"	9d—2¾"	16d—3½"	40d—5"	70d—7"
4d—1½"	7d—2¼"	10d—3"	20d—4"	50d—5½"	80d—8"

Nails and screws have different strengths and weaknesses. Screws typically offer better holding power, thanks to threads that grip the wood or other material, but most screws are relatively brittle and cannot bend far without breaking. Nails have relatively poor holding power (particularly standard nails) but offer greater shear strength than screws: they can bend without breaking. The holding power (and driving ease) of nails is increased by coating them with resin. These are called *cement-coated* (CC) nails, *resin-coated* nails, *coated sinkers* or *sinkers*, or *coolers*. Holding power also can be increased by various deformations, or threading, of the shaft, such as barbs, chemical etching, annular rings, spiral threads, or flutes. These nails are very difficult if not impossible to remove without damaging the wood, while screws are easily removed.

Plain common nails with no coating are called *bright*. Nails come in boxes, brown paper bags, and carded; the latter is the most expensive way to buy them. If you need a lot of nails, buy them in 25- or 30-pound boxes or kegs to save money.

NOTE:

Because of the increased holding power of coated or deformed nails, they are a little bit shorter than the same d-size common nail.

BUYING TIPS:

Choose the right nail material for outdoor use. Standard nails will quickly rust with weather exposure, and the wrong type of nail can "bleed" (leave dark streaks) onto wood fencing, decking, and trim. The best all-around material that's guaranteed not to rust or bleed is stainless steel, but it's expensive. Aluminum nails won't rust, but they can bleed on cedar and redwood and often are not strong enough for structural work. Hot-dipped galvanized nails are a reliable, economical option. They have a thick coating of zinc to resist corrosion combined with the strength of steel. However, galvanized nails will bleed on cedar and redwood (due to a chemical reaction with the wood), even when the project is painted. Galvanized nails with an electroplated coating offer much less corrosion-resistance than hot-dipped and should be used only where there is no direct exposure to weather. Finally, use only stainless-steel or hot-dipped galvanized nails with pressure-treated lumber. The chemical treatment in the wood will corrode other materials.

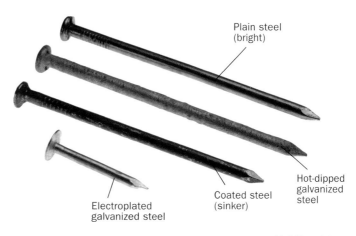

Plain steel (bright)

Hot-dipped galvanized steel

Coated steel (sinker)

Electroplated galvanized steel

Nail Materials.

Common Nail

DESCRIPTION:

Fairly thick with a large, round, flat head.

USE:

General construction work, such as framing and a wide variety of other purposes. Comes in many different sizes. Use common nails for structural applications.

USE TIPS:

When driving common nails with a hammer, try to snap your wrist rather than hitting the nail with arm power. If you are using cement-coated nails, do not stop hammering until the nail is driven all the way in. If you stop, the cement (which is actually a friction-sensitive glue) will set, and when you start again the nail might bend.

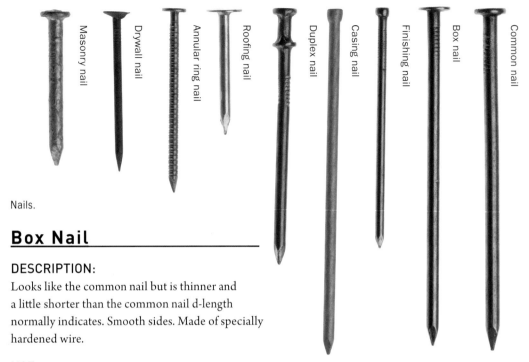

Masonry nail · Drywall nail · Annular ring nail · Roofing nail · Duplex nail · Casing nail · Finishing nail · Box nail · Common nail

Nails.

Box Nail

DESCRIPTION:

Looks like the common nail but is thinner and a little shorter than the common nail d-length normally indicates. Smooth sides. Made of specially hardened wire.

USE:

A variation on the common nail but with a thinner diameter (lighter gauge) and slightly blunted tip, making it good where there is a danger of the nail splitting thin wood, such as 1x lumber and exterior trim. Does not hold as well and is not as a strong as a common nail. Suitable for general, nonstructural applications.

Finishing Nail

ALSO KNOWN AS:

Finish nail, brad.

DESCRIPTION:

Thin, with a very small, cupped head. Comes in both very small and fairly long sizes and may be sized according to wire gauge (diameter) with a number from 12 down to 20 (the higher the number, the smaller the diameter) as well as by actual length and by the d system.

USE:

For wherever you don't want nail heads to show, such as when installing interior trim. The head is small and cupped so it can be easily countersunk, or driven beneath the wood surface, with a hammer and nail set. The hole is then filled with wood putty and sanded for a near-invisible finish.

Casing Nail

DESCRIPTION:

Looks like a large finishing nail but is thicker and has a flat rather than a cupped head.

USE:

This is a close cousin of the finishing nail and gets its name from its main use: securing case molding and other rough trim. It is thicker and harder than a finishing nail, so you can use fewer of them.

Ringed, Threaded, or Barbed Nails

DESCRIPTIONS & USES:

Nails with shanks that have been shaped to have the greatest holding power possible:

ANNULAR RING NAIL:

Shank has many sharp ridges. Uses include underlayment, shingles, siding, and paneling. Typically used with finish materials such as paneling or siding.

DRYWALL NAIL:

Has a partially barbed or ringed shank and may be resin-coated; has a large, cupped head. Used for securing drywall panels to wood framing. A *plasterboard* or *lath nail* is another version of this, with a larger head and smaller barbs.

ROOFING NAIL:

Large head and a barbed shank, usually galvanized steel or aluminum. Used for securing asphalt shingles and building paper. Nails for metal roofing have a rubber or plastic washer under the head to create a water seal. *Cap nails* have a large plastic or metal washer; used for securing sheet materials, such as building paper (roofing felt) and housewrap.

SPIRAL NAIL:

Small head with a spiral shank. Traditionally used to install subflooring and some wood flooring but is much less commonly used today.

USE TIPS:

DRYWALL:

Hit it just hard enough so that the nail head dimples the surface paper but goes no deeper. Screws should generally be used with drywall.

ROOFING:

Comes in various sizes up to 1 ¼ inches. Carefully size the nail to the thickness of the roofing being fastened. Available in rust-resistant materials, such as aluminum or stainless steel. Strike as few times as possible to avoid scratching off the rust-resistant coating.

Cut Flooring Nail

DESCRIPTION:
Flat, tapered shank and head. Looks like old-fashioned, hand-forged nails.

USE:
For nailing into edges of floorboards without splintering (typically used with floor nailers) and for decorative purposes in restoration.

Duplex Nail

ALSO KNOWN AS:
Duplex head nail, sprig nail, double-head scaffold nail, staging nail.

DESCRIPTION:
Regular common nail with a second head (ring) about ¼ inch below the top head.

USE:
For temporary work, such as scaffolding and concrete forms. You drive it in up to the first head like a normal nail but can easily remove it by pulling on the top head.

Panel Nail

DESCRIPTION:
Decorative brads available in a variety of colors. Some come with annular rings for better holding power.

USE:
Securing wood paneling to wall when nails are to be inconspicuous.

Masonry Nail

ALSO KNOWN AS:
Concrete nail.

DESCRIPTION:
Looks like a thick common nail but is made of case-hardened and tempered steel. Its shank comes four ways: *round*, *fluted* (or knurled), *flat* (cut), or *square*. The cut-type masonry nail looks like an old-fashioned cut nail. Another version is the *hammer drive pin*, a hardened-steel pin inside a ¼-inch-diameter flanged sleeve—the sleeve is inserted into a predrilled hole, then the pin is driven with a hammer to expand and secure the sleeve in the hole.

USE:

Securing items such as electrical conduit furring strips to masonry (brick, concrete, block, etc.), where great holding power is not needed. Hammered in.

USE TIPS:

Use a 2-pound or bricklayer's hammer to drive these nails. Wear safety glasses to protect against flying masonry chips, and use as few blows as possible.

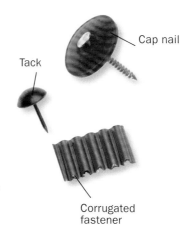

Cap nail

Tack

Corrugated fastener

Tack

TYPES:

Common tack, ornamental, or ornamental tack

DESCRIPTION & USE:

COMMON TACK:

Short, flat- or round-sided nail, some with an extra sharp "cut" end. Mainly used for securing carpeting.

ORNAMENTAL:

Has a tack-like shaft, or shank, and a large, fancy head, often mushroom-shaped. Used for securing upholstery.

USE TIPS:

Available with a blued finish or in copper and aluminum. The latter are impervious to weather and are good for boating applications but also for securing webbing on outdoor furniture. Starting tacks without a small-headed hammer, such as a tack hammer, is difficult but can be done by holding the tack with a hairpin or needlenose pliers instead of your fingers.

Corrugated Fastener

ALSO KNOWN AS:

Corrugated nail.

DESCRIPTION:

Short, wide, wavy piece of thin metal with one sharpened edge.

USE:

Nailed across miter joints, such as in picture frames and boxes.

CHAPTER 2

SCREWS

ABOUT SCREWS

Screws have developed in performance and popularity over the years, and have gradually supplanted nails for many household applications, including decking, drywall, subflooring, cabinetry, fencing, and many general construction tasks. Where once a hobbyist might have reached for some box or finishing nails to assemble a simple utility cabinet or set of shelves, he or she now is more likely to use drywall screws instead. The primary advantage of screws is that they hold better than most nails and resist pulling out, which means fewer squeaks in floors due to loose subflooring, ceiling drywall that doesn't droop as much over time, and decking boards that stay flatter. Screws also are easier to install in many situations (particularly for beginners), and they're much easier to remove than nails without damaging the host materials.

Screws typically are driven with screwdrivers (or screw tips on power drills), except for lag screws, which are driven with a wrench. Most screws are pointed and tapered (unlike *bolts*, which have blunt ends and are straight), except for machine screws, which are actually bolts. Still with us?

When selecting a screw for a job, a number of factors come into play: length, gauge (diameter), material, head style, drive type, and thread, as follows:

LENGTH:

Screws range in size from ¼ inch up to around 6 inches long. Note that length typically is measured from the point (tip) of the screw to the level where the screw head meets the material the screw is installed in. For example, a deck screw is installed flush (or slightly deeper than flush) with decking, so the screw is measured from the top of the head to the point. A standard sheet metal screw's head sits on the surface of the metal, so its length is measured from the bottom of the head to the screw point.

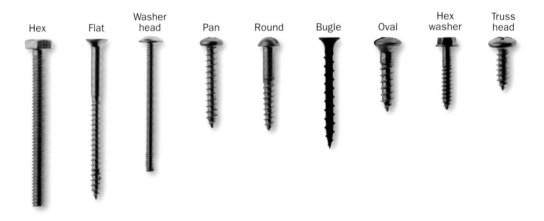

Hex   Flat   Washer head   Pan   Round   Bugle   Oval   Hex washer   Truss head

Screw head styles.

GAUGE:

The diameter of the unthreaded shank under the screw head is described according to numbers commonly ranging from No. (or #) 5 to No. 14, with the higher number being the larger. The total range is No. 2 to No. 24. A No. 5 screw is about ⅛ inch in diameter. Screws of the same gauge are available in different lengths. Always order a screw by length and number: ½-inch No. 8, for example.

MATERIAL:

Most screws are made with steel and may be plain steel or coated with various metals or other materials for corrosion-resistance. Common types include coated (as in deck screws), galvanized, zinc-plated, brass-plated, and chrome-plated. There are also stainless-steel and solid-brass screws, both of which are essentially rust-proof but can cause other metals to corrode when the dissimilar metals come into contact. For outdoor use, screws must be stainless steel (or brass) or galvanized or otherwise coated for corrosion resistance. Bleeding (see page 11) is likely to occur on cedar and redwood if the screws aren't stainless steel or specially coated and guaranteed not to bleed on these natural woods.

HEAD STYLE:

The shape of the screw head. In truth, there are too many shapes to describe here, but the photo (page 76) shows the most common head styles. Generally, screw heads that are flat on the bottom are intended to sit on top of the receiving material. Heads that are beveled or conical on the bottom are designed to embed into the material, so the top of the head is flush with the surface.

DRIVE TYPE:

Screw drive types.

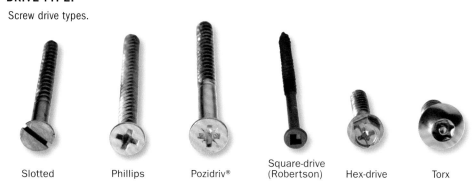

| Slotted | Phillips | Pozidriv® | Square-drive (Robertson) | Hex-drive | Torx |

Refers to the shape of the screwdriver or screw tip used to drive the screw. The most common are the *slotted* (straight slot) and *Phillips* (cross-shaped slot), but there are several others, all of which perform better than the two historic standards. These include *Pozidriv®*, *square-drive* (Robertson), *hex-drive* (Allen), and *Torx* (star-drive). It's important that you match up not only the right screw tip with the screw but also the right *size* of screw tip. For example, square-drive, Pozidriv®, and even the old standby Phillips-drive come in five or more different sizes, but the most common are 1, 2, and 3. Torx and hex-drive screws come in many sizes.

THREADS:

Screw threads vary by depth (how deep the grooves are), pitch (how steeply they spiral up the screw shank), and spacing (how far apart they are). Threads also can run all the way from the point to the head or stop somewhere short of the head, leaving a smooth shank that slides through the first host material to help pull it against the mating material that receives the screw threads. Thread specifications are simpler for wood screws and other basic construction screws than they are for machine screws and bolts and may simply be designated as "coarse" or "fine," or by a threads-per-inch (TPI) count. Since screws go into material rather than nuts or threaded holes, the thread should be suited for the intended material.

USE TIP:

Phillips and Pozidriv screws look almost the same at a glance, but they perform differently and require different screw tips. Phillips have a simple cross-shaped drive slot, usually with no additional markings. Pozidriv have a cross-shaped slot with a square center and four additional indentations around the cross, each indicated by a tick mark. Pozidriv® screw tips have a shape to match, with a square center and four tapered ridges that fit into the additional indentations. These give the Pozidriv superior grip over Phillips screws, to minimize stripping and provide more driving power. A Phillips tip works, if poorly, in a Pozidriv screw, but a Pozidriv® tip doesn't fit in a Phillips screw head. Phillips tips are marked with a size number and the letters "PH." Pozidriv® have a number and the letters "PZ."

Standard Wood Screw

DESCRIPTION:

Threads along about three-fourths of a tapered shaft, with a variety of head styles. Most common material is zinc chromate-treated steel. Commonly sold 100 to a box, as well as in smaller and larger containers.

USE:

Securing wood items to one another. Generally, *oval-* and *flat-head* screws are used when countersinking for decorative purposes or with hardware such as hinges, but an oval head is generally easier to remove and slightly better-looking. *Round-head screws* are used with thin woods and with washers.

Wood screw.

USE TIPS:

Use coarse-thread wood screws for softwoods and fine-thread screws for most hardwoods. Traditional wood screws still have a place in some woodworking and furniture-making applications and for installing hinges and other hardware, but they have been replaced by other types of wood screws, such as deck screws, drywall screws, and multi-material screws, for many general construction projects. Slot-head wood screws should be avoided unless the single slot is desired for aesthetics or you're using very small screws that can be driven by hand with a regular screwdriver. Finishing screws (page 19) and pocket screws (page 19) are two variations on the conventional wood screw that offer specific advantages.

Finishing Screw

ALSO KNOWN AS:

Trim-head screw.

Finishing screw.

DESCRIPTION:

Essentially the screw version of a
finishing nail (page 12). Its slender shank is designed for fine or thin wood finish materials, and its small, rounded head countersinks cleanly into the material, leaving only a small hole. Typically Torx or square-drive.

USE:

Installing trim, assembling cabinets, and other finish work in wood.

USE TIPS:

Use finishing screws where appearance counts and when you need more holding power than a finishing nail can provide. Drill pilot holes to prevent splitting the wood and to aid countersinking, particularly in hardwood.

Pocket Screw

ALSO KNOWN AS:

Pocket-hole screw.

DESCRIPTION:

Specialty wood screw for pocket-hole joints. Partial threading helps pull mating pieces tightly together. Washer head helps create a tight joint and prevents the head from sinking into soft or fragile materials, such as particleboard.

Pocket screws.

USE:

Wood-to-wood connections employing pocket holes—steeply angled pilot holes drilled through the face of one piece and into the edge or end grain of the mating piece.

USE TIPS:

A pocket-hole joint hides the fasteners on the inside or underside of the assembly and creates a stronger connection than screws driven at right angles to the joint. Pocket holes have long been a secret weapon of furniture makers and woodworkers but now are popular among hobbyists and DIYers. Pocket screws cost more than conventional wood screws but are worth their weight in gold when performance counts.

Drywall Screw

DESCRIPTION:
Thin, straight, blued (looks black) screw with deep threads, especially sharp point, and a flat Phillips head (actually a special design called a *bugle head*, which prevents tearing the surface paper of drywall). Self-tapping—needs no predrilled hole in soft materials. There are two kinds—fine thread for metal studs and coarse thread for wooden studs. Some drywall screws for metal studs are *self-drilling* and have a tiny drill-bit-like tip for cutting a starter hole into light-gauge metal framing.

USE:
Securing drywall or wood to wood or metal (stud framing, beams, furring, or joists).

USE TIPS:
Drywall screws are the only type to use for installing drywall, but they also work quite well for general wood construction projects, provided the project is non-structural and not outdoors. Drywall screws are relatively weak and very brittle (they can't bend without breaking), and they're not corrosion-resistant.

Fine

Coarse

Drywall screws.

Deck Screw

DESCRIPTION:
Thin wood screw with deep, sharp threads designed to penetrate lumber without a pilot hole. Similar to a coarse-thread drywall screw, but stronger and less brittle. Either stainless steel or galvanized, or otherwise coated for corrosion-resistance.

USE:
Wood deck construction and almost any other outdoor wood project.

BUYING TIPS:
Check the screw material carefully for each application. Many types, including galvanized, will bleed onto cedar and redwood (see page 11). Deck screws with special coatings are corrosion-resistant only when the coating remains intact; quality counts. Hot-dipped galvanized and stainless-steel screws are suitable for use in pressure-treated lumber (the standard material for deck understructures); most coated screws are not.

Deck screw.

Multi-Material Screw

DESCRIPTION:

Variety of premium screws optimized for wood and other materials and a range of applications. SPAX is one common brand and includes special features, such as serrated threads that cut into wood to minimize splitting and ease driving and ridged heads that create their own countersink holes to help bury the head flush.

USE:

Specialty applications where conventional wood, deck, or drywall screws are problematic. Versions for wood are excellent for screwing into the edges of plywood. Types designed for MDF, particleboard, and plastic hold better than conventional screws.

BUYING TIPS:

Basically a better mousetrap. Not always worth the extra cost, but can make a difference in certain applications. Choose the right screw for the materials and conditions. Some can be used outdoors and in masonry.

Multi-material screw.

Lag Screw

ALSO KNOWN AS:

Lag bolt, or simply "lag."

Lag screw.

DESCRIPTION:

Heavy-duty wood screw with coarse threads and a large, nut-like head driven with a socket wrench (or power drill with socket).

USE:

Structural connections for wood framing, such as on a deck, arbor, play structure, fence, or outdoor furniture.

USE TIP:

Drill a *pilot* hole for the threaded portion of the lag and a *clearance* hole for the shank to ease driving and prevent splitting the wood. If desired, also drill a countersink hole for recessing the head (and washer). Always use a washer for soft woods and all structural wood connections to prevent the head from tearing and sinking into the wood, which compromises both appearance and strength. For structural connections where you have access to both sides of the adjoining members, a carriage bolt (page 27) provides a stronger connection than a lag screw.

BUYING TIPS:

Lag screws are typically used outdoors, but not all are equally corrosion-resistant. Shiny, zinc-plated lags usually offer less protection than hot-dipped galvanized versions. Stainless steel, as usual, is the gold standard.

Timber Screw

ALSO KNOWN AS:

Heavy-duty wood screw, ledger screw.

Timber screw.

DESCRIPTION:

High-strength, often very long, wood screw with coarse threads along the first few inches of the screw's shank. Typically with washered head, either hex head (for driving with a drill and hex-drive attachment) or Torx-drive.

USE:

Structural framing connections in wood. Used in place of lag screws in some applications and in place of common nails in others. Commonly used for joining roof rafters or trusses to wall frames, fastening landscape timbers, and building decks and other outdoor framed structures. Some are code-approved for installing deck ledger boards.

USE TIPS:

Timber screws can replace lag screws and even wood framing connectors in some applications, but always confirm their use with the project designer/engineer and the local building code, as applicable.

Sheet Metal Screw

DESCRIPTION:

Similar to a wood screw but threaded along entire length of shank. Wide variety of head-styles, including flat, oval, pan, hex, and washered hex (and others). Most are self-tapping, while some are self-drilling (with a drill-bit-like screw tip). Versions for metal roofing have neoprene washers or gaskets under the head to create a waterproof seal.

Sheet metal screws.

USE:

Fastening thin metal to thin metal. Longer versions typically hold pretty well in wood as well as metal.

USE TIP:

Be careful not to over-tighten screws in thin metal, as the self-tapped holes strip easily. The screw stays in place, but the connection might not be tight.

Concrete Screw

DESCRIPTION:

Hardened-steel screw with either tapered flat head or hex washer head; coated against corrosion. *Hi-low* threads have alternating deep and shallow thread channels for better grip in hard materials. Often sold with special carbide-tipped masonry drill bit for drilling pilot holes. Available in ¼- and ⅜-inch diameters and a variety of lengths.

USE:

Screws directly into concrete, brick, mortar, and other masonry materials without the need for an anchor sleeve or other device. Ideal for attaching wood and other materials to concrete and masonry, and for mounting items to masonry walls.

USE TIPS:

Always drill an appropriately sized pilot hole, as specified by the manufacturer. Make sure holes are deep enough, and blow them out with air to remove dust and debris. A shallow or partially filled hole will stop your screw short.

Concrete screw.

Cementboard Screw

DESCRIPTION:

Similar to a concrete screw, with hi-low threads and a corrosion-resistant coating. Flat head for flush installation, often with ridges below head for cutting a countersink hole.

USE:

Installing cementboard to walls and floors. Worth the extra cost for a quality tile installation. Screws install cleanly without pilot holes and minimize damage to brittle cementboard. Hold better than galvanized roofing nails and are strong and corrosion-resistant (unlike drywall screws).

Cementboard screw.

Screw Washers

DESCRIPTION:

Small metal circles that come in three shapes: *flat*, *countersunk* (slightly cone-shaped), and *flush* (slightly funnel-shaped). The latter two are known as *finishing washers*. Size matches screw being used.

Countersunk finishing washers.

USE:

Washers provide a hard surface for a screw to be tightened against, thereby preventing damage to the surface and allowing a tighter fit. Countersunk (for oval-head screws) and flush (for flat-head screws) are more attractive as well. Flat washers are for use with round-head screws.

Dowel Screw

DESCRIPTION:
Essentially a two-pointed lag screw, often with a flat-faceted center section for turning the fastener. A similar item is the hanger bolt (page 42).

Dowel screw.

USE:
Hidden fastener for furniture assembly, hanging wood items from ceilings, and installing wood finials on stair newels and other wood posts.

Gutter Screw

DESCRIPTION:
Very long (about 7 inches) screw with partial wood-screw threads and a hex- or square-drive head. Commonly sold with a special hanger bracket or a gutter ferrule—a long metal cylinder through which the gutter screw is driven.

USE:
Replacing loose/missing gutter spikes or other hangers on conventional metal gutters.

USE TIPS:
Gutter screws are easier to install than traditional spikes (with ferrules) and can be driven anywhere along a fascia board (the wide trim board behind gutters, covering the ends of the roof rafters).

BUYING TIPS:
Metal ferrules are more durable than plastic ferrules. Hangers are good for lifting gutters that sag along the front (outside) edge.

Gutter screw with bracket.

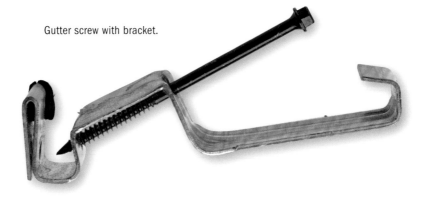

CHAPTER 3

NUTS & BOLTS

ABOUT NUTS & BOLTS

Bolts have a lot in common with screws, but there are several ways to tell them apart. While screws are driven into virgin material (or into pilot holes drilled into virgin material), bolts are mated with nuts or with threaded holes in the host material. Screws have sharp points, tapered shanks, and steeply pitched threads for burrowing into material; bolts have blunt ends, shanks without taper, and fine threads (typically) that must match their mating nut or threaded hole. Threads on bolts are universally called *machine threads*, distinguishing them from the *wood-screw threads* found on most screws.

Bolt diameters are noted in inches or millimeters, and thread size follows accordingly. When a bolt diameter is given in inches (standard US system), the thread count is measured in *threads per inch* (TPI). For example, a ¼-inch × 20 bolt is ¼ inch long and has 20 threads per inch. The higher the TPI count, the finer the threads. Alternatively, when the bolt diameter is given in millimeters (metric units), the thread size is indicated by *thread pitch*, or how far apart the threads are from one another. The standard thread pitch for a 7mm bolt, for example, is 1mm, meaning the threads are spaced 1mm apart.

However, even if you know all of this about bolt size and threading, there's no guarantee you'll get the right bolt and nut simply using the number system, because the notation isn't always consistent among manufacturers and suppliers. It's best to test-fit bolts and nuts in the store, and if you have a bolt that you have to match, bring it with you to make sure everything fits. Hardware stores often have bolt-thread displays with threaded inserts into which you can thread your bolt to learn its diameter and thread configuration.

Machine Bolt

TYPES:

Hex bolt
Tap bolt
Flange bolt

DESCRIPTION & USE:

Used primarily for assembling metal parts. The main types have slightly different features:

HEX BOLT:
Partially threaded shank with a flat end and either a square or hex head. The standard, classic bolt.

TAP BOLT:
Similar to a hex bolt but with a fully threaded shank.

FLANGE BOLT:
Similar to a hex bolt but with a smaller hex head with a flange underneath to serve as a washer.

There are several ways to keep nuts from coming off of bolts because of vibration, such as on machinery: the "double-nut" technique (two nuts per bolt); using a locknut (page 31); using a lock washer, either the split-ring type or the internal-tooth type (page 32); or using anaerobic adhesive (page 71), a type of adhesive that comes in small plastic tubes, one drop of which hardens inside the threads.

Carriage bolts (page 27) and machine bolts come with *rolled* or *cut* threads, but the cut thread is better. Here the thread is cut directly into the steel shaft used for the bolt, while the rolled thread is added separately after the shaft is machined. The rolled-thread type uses less metal. In smaller sizes this may not matter, but in larger sizes the shank part of the bolt may match the drilled hole perfectly but the rolled or threaded part may not. The result is a sloppy fit.

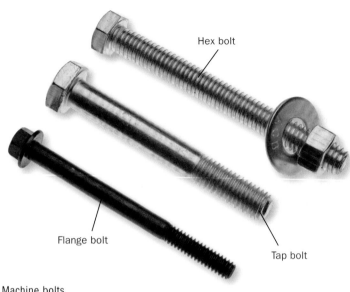

Hex bolt

Flange bolt

Tap bolt

Machine bolts.

Machine Screw

DESCRIPTION:

Threaded along its entire length, it has a flat tip and a round or flat head, and is designed primarily to be screwed into prethreaded holes in metal, though of course it works with nuts too. Actually a type of bolt, although it is driven with a screwdriver instead of a wrench.

Machine screw threads commonly come in two sizes: coarse (24 TPI) and fine (32 TPI). When a screw is specified (such as in electrical work) as a 6-32 screw, what is meant is a 6-gauge diameter, or No. 6 size, with fine threads. The length should be given in inches after the size, as in 6-32 × ¾ inch.

Machine screw.

BUYING TIPS:

Most electrical boxes need 8-32 machine screws.

Stove Bolt

DESCRIPTION:
Usually threaded its entire length, with a round or flat head that has a straight screw slot; driven with a screwdriver. The most often used sizes (diameters) are ⅛, ⁵⁄₃₂, and ³⁄₁₆ inches. Exactly the same item as a machine screw (page 26), the difference being that stove bolts are supplied to the customer with nuts and intended for use with nuts, while the machine screw is intended for use in prethreaded holes in metal (shown with a square nut).

USE:
Light assembly (such as basic kitchen appliances), because a screwdriver has less tightening power than a wrench.

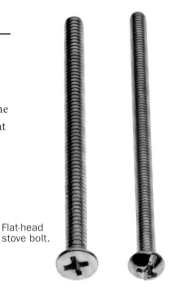

Flat-head
stove bolt.

Round-head
stove bolt.

Carriage Bolt

ALSO KNOWN AS:
Carriage screw.

DESCRIPTION:
A large bolt, partially threaded, with a smooth, rounded head that has a square-sided portion just beneath it. That square part cuts into wood as the nut is tightened and resists the turning motion. A similar but smaller version is the *ribbed bolt*.

USE:
Used in wood where particular strength is required, where you will not be able to reach the head with a wrench, or where you do not want a turnable head exposed (there is no slot in the oval head).

USE TIPS:
Use washers under the nut on carriage bolts where the wood is very soft and you don't want the nut to dig in and cause damage, such as in outdoor redwood furniture. Also use a washer for all structural connections, such as in deck construction.

BUYING TIPS:
Carriage bolts used outdoors must be corrosion-resistant. Hot-dipped galvanized (slightly rough; dull gray) is the economical standard and offers better corrosion-resistance than

Carriage bolt.

zinc-plated (smooth; shinier silver) bolts. The nuts must also be hot-dipped galvanized because they are sized slightly larger to accommodate the thick galvanized coating on the bolts. Stainless steel is a more expensive option for carriage bolts but is usually overkill for standard building projects.

Socket Screw

DESCRIPTION:
Similar to a machine screw or machine bolt, depending on its size, but with a socket head that accepts an Allen wrench. A *socket-head capscrew* has a cylindrical head, typically knurled on the outside. Other types of socket screws have a button head or a flat head, the latter for mounting flush with the host material.

Socket-head capscrew.

USE:
Securing metal parts, with raised or flush installation.

Setscrew

DESCRIPTION:
Typically small, short cylinder threaded along its entire length. One end tapered to a blunt point; the other end with a hex-shaped recess for accepting an Allen wrench. Headless design allows a setscrew to be driven all the way into a threaded hole for a flush installation, with no head protruding above the finished surface.

Setscrew.

USE:
Used to secure an outer element to an inner element, such as a shaft. Faucet handles and spouts, doorknobs, and metal collars are commonly fastened to other parts with setscrews, which are hidden inside their own threaded holes.

USE TIPS:
If it's not obvious how a metal part is joined to another metal part—that is, there are no visible bolts, clamps, screw heads, etc.—there's a good chance they're joined by a setscrew. Look for a small hole in an inconspicuous area of the outer part, then insert different Allen wrenches into the hole until you find the right fit.

Sex Bolts

ALSO KNOWN AS:
Chicago bolts, barrel nuts.

DESCRIPTION:
Mating bolt-and-nut pair with male and female halves. Female half has a broad, flat head attached to a cylinder with interior threads. Male half is a machine bolt with a similarly broad, flat head. Either head may be slotted or recessed with a variety of drive types. Available in a range of lengths. Some heads have serrated undersides for increased holding power.

Sex bolts.

USE:
Joining a variety of items and materials, particularly when a finished look and easy disassembly are desired.

USE TIPS:
One of the handiest bolts you've never heard of (or given much notice). Sex bolts are great for craft projects, such as hand-bound books and photo albums, where a conventional bolt and nut would ruin the aesthetics. The threaded cylinder and bolt allow for some adjustability to accommodate different material thicknesses.

U-Bolts & J-Bolts

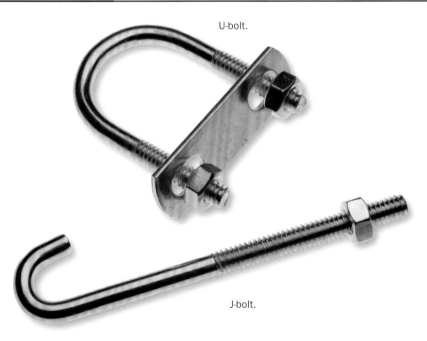

U-bolt.

J-bolt.

DESCRIPTION:

Threaded steel rod bent into either a U or J shape (rounded or squared off). The most useful U-bolt has a slotted bar across both ends that clamps down as the nuts are tightened. A very small version with a large cast-metal piece across the opening is used for clamping cable ends.

USE:

Clamping odd shapes or hanging items, or creating tie-down anchors. Often used in conjunction with *S-hooks* and *8-hooks* (figure-8-shaped steel pieces). Some large J-bolts are actually L-shaped, and are designed for embedding into concrete foundations and deck footings for anchoring wood framing members and metal post bases.

Threaded Rod

ALSO KNOWN AS:

All thread.

DESCRIPTION:

Metal rod threaded along its entire length. Commonly available in lengths 2 feet and longer and in the following diameters: 3/16, 1/4, 5/16, 3/8, and 1/2 inches. Much larger sizes can also be obtained on special order. Think of it as an infinitely long bolt.

Rod may be made of stainless steel, plain steel, electroplated, zinc-plated, and hot-dipped galvanized. Stainless steel and hot-dipped galvanized are suitable for outdoor use.

USE:

Used with nuts and washers for many different jobs: hanging, bracing, fastening, supporting, and mounting. Also useful where a bolt doesn't have sufficient threads to work. For example, a 6-inch bolt may have only 1½ inches of thread; a threaded rod will have sufficient threads.

USE TIPS:

To avoid burrs when cutting the rod (it may be cut with a hacksaw or bolt cutters), make the cut between two nuts, then turn the nuts off the cut ends to remove the burrs. Cut ends can be sharp; either file them smooth (after installing all nuts) or cover ends with a cap nut (page 31). Join lengths of threaded rod end-to-end with a coupling nut (page 32).

Miscellaneous Nuts

Hex nut.

Square nut.

Locknut.

Flange nut.

Jam nut.

Cap nut.

Axle nut (threaded).

Axle cap nut (press-on).

Wing nut.

Slotted nut.

Coupling nut.

DESCRIPTION:

HEX:
Standard six-sided nut.

SQUARE:
Similar to hex nut but with only four sides.

JAM:
Thin hex nut. Sometimes used in conjunction with hex nuts to lock the two together.

FLANGE:
Hex nut with flanged bottom to serve as washer.

LOCKNUT:
Hex nut with a plastic insert to prevent unintended loosening. Maintains tension even when vibrated repeatedly, such as on machinery.

CAP:
Closed-end nut with a smooth rounded or pointed dome for finished appearance and/or safety. Also called *acorn nut*, particularly when cap is pointed.

AXLE:
Two versions: Stamped, unthreaded cap that is pressed or hammered onto the end of an axle to secure a wheel on a wagon, baby carriage, cart, etc., and a threaded version with a center hole so a small axle shaft can extend through the nut.

WING:

Two upward-projecting wings flanking a threaded middle. Good for light use when something needs to be regularly disassembled by hand. Not intended for use with wrenches.

SLOTTED NUT:

Also called a *castle nut*. Hex nut with notched top edge for accepting a cotter pin (page 44) inserted through hole in bolt or axle. Pin prevents nut from turning.

COUPLING:

Long, six-sided nut used to join two lengths of threaded rod.

Nut & Bolt Washers

DESCRIPTION:

Fender washer.

FLAT:

Flat, circular shape, available in various thicknesses and with a range of inner and outer diameters. Smaller sizes provide a smooth surface for a nut or bolt head to be tightened against. Washers also prevent bolt heads and nuts from digging into wood and other materials.

Flat washer.

FENDER:

Common term for flat washers with large outer diameters.

SPLIT-RING LOCK:

Spring action of slight spiral creates pressure that keeps a nut from loosening. Typically used with metal materials.

Split-ring lock washer.

INTERNAL-TOOTH LOCK:

Many small teeth pointing in toward hole serve to keep nut from loosening.

Internal-tooth lock washer.

EXTERNAL-TOOTH LOCK:

Many small teeth pointing outward that serve to keep nut from loosening. Can be used with wood screws.

External-tooth lock washer.

SEALING WASHER:

Flat metal washer with a bonded rubber gasket to create a watertight seal around bolt or screw hole.

Sealing washer.

CHAPTER 4

WALL ANCHORS
& HANGING HARDWARE

ABOUT WALL ANCHORS

Wall anchors, or fasteners, are particularly useful on two kinds of wall construction: hollow wall (usually drywall), if there is no stud or solid material to simply drive a screw or nail into; and hardwall, such as plaster or masonry, where the wall material is too hard for screws to take hold in. Wall anchors come in a variety of sizes and types, and new designs and brand names appear often. Be sure to check all your sources for the best ones available in your area. Below are some of the most popular types, which fall into three categories: *light duty*, for any kind of wall; *masonry*; and *hollow-wall fasteners*.

Plastic Expansion Anchor

ALSO KNOWN AS:
Light-duty wall anchor, tubular anchor, plastic anchor, hollow anchor, plastic shield.

DESCRIPTION:
Cone-shaped or cylindrical plastic sheaths of various sizes corresponding to various-sized screws. They expand against the sides of the hole when the screw is driven into them.

USE:
Anchoring wood screws in drywall, plaster, or masonry. They are inserted into a predrilled hole and tapped flush with a hammer.

Plastic expansion anchor.

USE TIPS:
The hole must be just the right size—too big and the anchor won't hold, too small and it won't go in far enough to work. Use these anchors for hanging lightweight objects only. Also use them only for objects that hang straight down, as they provide very little pullout resistance.

Threaded Drywall Anchor

ALSO KNOWN AS:
Screw-in wall anchor, self-drilling anchor.

DESCRIPTION:
Screw-like anchor with oversize threads and a double-pointed tip for burrowing into drywall without a pilot hole. Made of metal or hard plastic. Butt end has cross-slots for Phillips screw tip, used for installing anchor.

USE:
Hanging lightweight items from drywall. Does not work well on plaster or other materials.

USE TIPS:
These light-duty, hollow-wall anchors can handle a little more weight and offer somewhat more pullout resistance than plastic expansion anchors (page 33), but they are still suitable only for lightweight items. Use a screwdriver or drill to drive them directly into drywall, applying heavy pressure and stopping when the anchor is flush with the surface.

BUYING TIPS:
Most anchors are designed to accept a #6 or #8 sheet metal screw, and screws often are packaged with the anchors. Buy metal anchors whenever possible. Plastic versions are weak and can easily break or twist out of shape.

Threaded drywall anchor.

Toggle Bolt & Anchor

ALSO KNOWN AS:
Toggles, spring-wing toggle, umbrella bolt.

DESCRIPTION:
Typically, a machine screw threaded into a set of collapsible "wings." One type has spring-loaded wings that squeeze together to fit through the installation hole, which then open up when they reach the open space behind the drywall; the other type uses gravity. The wings are pulled against the backside of the drywall when the machine screw is tightened from the front side of the wall. Suitable for hanging a wide range of items from drywall and plaster.

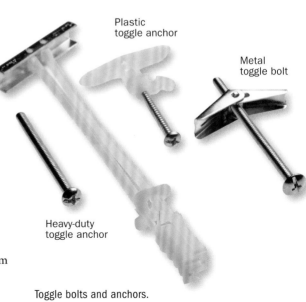

Plastic toggle anchor

Metal toggle bolt

Heavy-duty toggle anchor

Toggle bolts and anchors.

Most toggles are metal, but there are plastic versions with wings that are activated when a screw is driven into the anchor; these generally are lighter-duty than most metal toggles. Some heavy-duty toggles have a solid bar that you pivot into position (parallel to the wall surface) after inserting it through the hole.

USE:

Hanging heavy items on drywall and plaster walls and ceilings. In drywall and plaster, toggles are far superior to plastic expansion and threaded anchors.

USE TIPS:

Note that the toggle will drop if the bolt is removed, and large holes are required to fit the wings through the wall material.

BUYING TIPS:

The toggle's machine screw must be inserted through the item you're hanging before you thread the wings onto the screw. Make sure the screw is long enough to accommodate the thickness of the item *plus* the drywall thickness (or plaster *and* lath thickness) *plus* the length of the wings when collapsed. If the screw isn't long enough, the wings won't reach into the open space behind the wall and therefore won't open up; the toggle will pull right out when tightened.

Molly Bolt

NOTE:

Molly bolt has become incorrectly used as a generic household term for toggle bolts and other types of hollow-wall anchors, but this is not accurate.

DESCRIPTION:

Molly bolt.

Consists of a machine screw built into a metal sleeve with wings that bend outward as the screw is tightened. A similar but smaller model, called a *jack nut*, is made for anchoring into hollow doors. Some brands have a plastic-tipped model that is hammered into drywall like a nail and then screwed tight.

USE:

Fastening medium-weight items to drywall and plaster walls. Provides more pullout resistance than expanding plastic and threaded drywall anchors, but not as much as toggle bolts.

USE TIPS:

Drill a clean, solid hole so the anchor can be anchored tightly in it and not turn around as you turn the screw. The anchor will remain in place even if the screw is removed, making it slightly more convenient than a toggle (page 34). A small wrench, a V-shaped wire device, is sometimes supplied to keep the sleeve from turning as you tighten the bolt.

Expansion Shield

ALSO KNOWN AS:
Lead shield, lag shield.

DESCRIPTION:
The most common type consists of a thick, slotted metal sleeve, usually made of lead. There is a one-piece design for use with wood screws and a two-piece design for use with lag bolts (most popular) and machine bolts. Another version, a *hammer drive pin*, is a nail-like device that is hammered in place. The shield expands slightly against the hole as the screw is driven into it.

Expansion shield.

USE:
For anchoring items into brick, concrete block, and concrete.

USE TIPS:
Bear in mind that these shields require very large holes to be drilled in masonry. You need a power drill and a masonry bit or, preferably, a hammer drill and bit, to make such holes, and alignment is not always easy. An alternative may be to use simple masonry nails (page 14) and furring strips (thin boards). If you are putting up a large job with furring strips, you may want to rent or buy a powder-actuated nailer—a nail gun that fires hardened pins into masonry.

Wedge Anchor

ALSO KNOWN AS:
Concrete wedge anchor.

DESCRIPTION:
Large bolt with machine threads over most of its length, smooth and flared at bottom end with a collar that is expanded by the flared end. Washer and nut at top end.

Wedge anchor.

USE:
Heavy-duty anchor for solid concrete. Anchor is inserted into predrilled hole.
When the nut is tightened, the flared bottom end pulls up against the collar, locking the anchor in the hole. Anchor cannot be removed once it is tightened.

Picture-Hanging Hardware

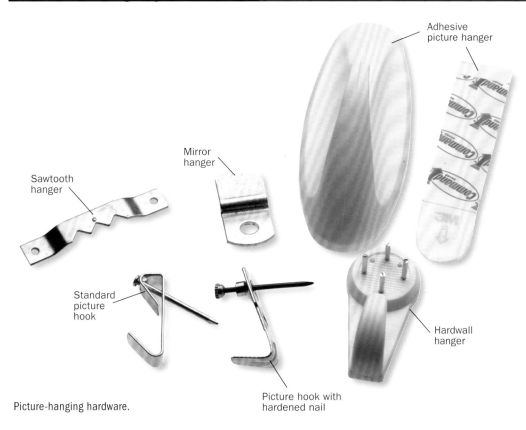

Picture-hanging hardware.

Labels on figure:
- Sawtooth hanger
- Mirror hanger
- Adhesive picture hanger
- Standard picture hook
- Picture hook with hardened nail
- Hardwall hanger

DESCRIPTION:

PICTURE HOOKS:

Metal hooks with holes for driving nails through at an angle. Come in various sizes and weight ratings, and in plain and ornamental styles. Standard types are best for drywall. Types with special hardened nails (sometimes with a knurled head for easy removal) are less likely to chip plaster walls.

ADJUSTABLE SAWTOOTH HANGER:

Strip of metal with serrations on one edge, nailed onto wood picture frame or screwed into plastic or wood items.

ADHESIVE PICTURE HANGER:

Hook or other device secured with a strip of adhesive. Adhesive is typically removable and is suitable for a range of hard surfaces.

HARDWALL HANGER:

Picture hook with special pins capable of being driven into hard material, such as masonry and plaster. Three-pin versions are standard, while larger four-pin hangers are heavier duty.

MIRROR HANGER:

Small offset clip with screw hole in one end.

USE:

Hanging pictures, mirrors, etc. of various weights.

USE TIPS:

Picture hooks typically needn't be driven into studs. They may be secured directly to drywall, plaster, and wood materials. To keep plaster from flaking, a small piece of transparent tape can be applied to the area where the nail is to be driven.

French Cleat

DESCRIPTION:

Heavy-duty picture hanger consisting of two large metal strips that interlock. One strip mounts to wall and has an upward-facing lip; other strip mounts to picture (or other item) and has a downward-facing strip.

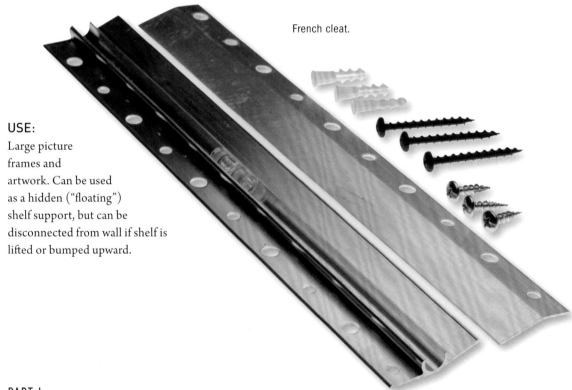

French cleat.

USE:

Large picture frames and artwork. Can be used as a hidden ("floating") shelf support, but can be disconnected from wall if shelf is lifted or bumped upward.

ABOUT SCREW EYES, SCREW HOOKS, EYE BOLTS & BOLT HOOKS

Haanging hooks and eyes with screw or bolt ends are available in a wide range of sizes, from cup hooks that you can install with your thumb and forefinger to heavy-duty eye bolts that might anchor a porch swing or a large chandelier. The critical factor to consider is the load rating, or how much weight the hardware can support. The hardware must have a *working* load rating that is higher than the weight of the item anchored by the hardware, including any additional loads or stresses placed on the hardware when the item is in use. And remember that any anchor is only as strong as the material it's anchored into.

Screw Eyes & Screw Hooks

DESCRIPTION:

Metal shaft with one end formed into a ring or a hook and the other threaded and pointed like a wood screw. Sizes range from tiny cup hooks to heavy pieces with shank diameters up to $5/8$ inch. Large versions are similar to a lag screw with a hook or eye end.

USE:

Hanging objects from walls, ceilings, and other horizontal and vertical wood structures. A range of specialty screw hooks are designed for specific uses:

CUP HOOK:
Small screw hook for hanging teacups and mugs by their handles. Also handy for hanging keys and other small items.

CEILING HOOK:
Somewhat decorative screw hook often used for hanging plants.

BICYCLE HOOK:
Large screw hook with plastic sheathing for hanging bicycles upside down from a garage ceiling.

UTILITY HOOK:
Similar to bicycle hook but larger and typically with squared corners. Sized for hanging ladders and other large—but not very heavy—tools and equipment.

SWAG HOOK:
Decorative hook anchor for hanging light fixtures (or their cords/chains) or plants. Screw-in versions have a wood-screw end; hollow-wall versions have a threaded bolt with a toggle-type anchor.

L-HOOK:
Hanging utensils, securing picture frames directly to walls (without hanging from a wire), holding curtain rods.

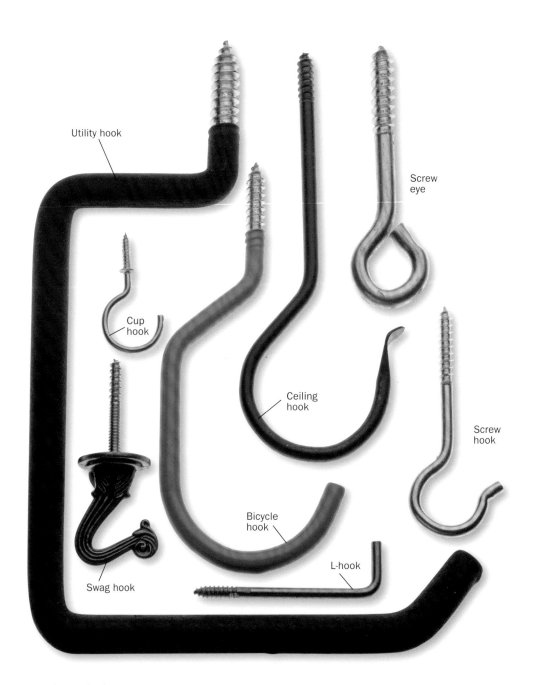

Utility hook

Screw eye

Cup hook

Ceiling hook

Screw hook

Bicycle hook

Swag hook

L-hook

Screw eyes and screw hooks.

USE TIPS:

All but the smallest screw eyes and hooks should be installed into pilot holes drilled into the receiving wood member. This ensures that you can drive the threads to full depth without excessive force and helps to prevent splitting the wood. Pilot hole diameters should be slightly smaller than the shank (not the threads) of the screw portion.

BUYING TIPS:

Most screw eyes and hooks are made with heavy metal wire bent into the desired shape. *Wire* screw eyes are identified by a slight gap at the base of the eye loop; these offer moderate strength at best. *Forged* screw eyes offer the highest load ratings and have a solid (continuous) eye made by forging the metal, not bending it.

Eye Bolts & Hook Bolts

DESCRIPTION:

Metal hook or eye (closed loop) with a machine-threaded bolt end for securing with a washer and nut. Sold in a wide range of sizes, shank diameters, and overall lengths.

USES:

Hanging items from horizontal or vertical supports made of metal, wood, or other suitable materials. Because bolts are inserted all the way through and are secured on the backside of the host member with a nut, they offer a much stronger connection than screw eyes or hooks, which rely solely on the grip of the screw threads.

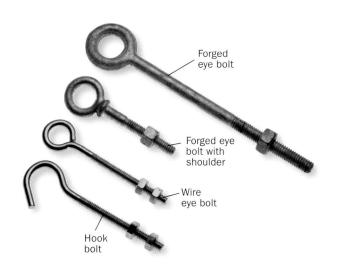

Forged
eye bolt

Forged eye
bolt with
shoulder

Wire
eye bolt

Hook
bolt

BUYING TIPS:

As with screw eyes, there are *wire* eye bolts and *forged* eye bolts. Wire bolts are bent into shape and do not have a continuous eye loop. They are not as strong as forged bolts. Some eye bolts can have very high load ratings, but note that most eye bolts are not designed for *angular* loads—loads that pulling on the eye at an angle, instead of pulling straight down. An eye bolt with a shoulder allows you to compress the material with the bolt without using a nut on the eye-end of the threads.

Hanger Bolt

DESCRIPTION:
Has coarse wood-screw threads on one end and bolt threads on the other, with a smooth portion in the middle.

Hanger bolt.

USE:
Commonly used to assemble commercial furniture. For do-it-yourselfers the hanger bolt is excellent for mounting in a joist or ceiling beam in order to hang fixtures.

Shelf Supports

TYPES:
Utility brackets
Standards & brackets
Pilasters & clips
Shelf pins
Floating shelf bracket

Utility bracket.

DESCRIPTION:

UTILITY BRACKETS:
Basic metal brackets with a center ridge and screw holes for securing to walls. One leg is longer than the other. Available in a range of sizes for various shelf depths.

CLOSET SHELF BRACKET:
Triangular metal bracket with a hook from the front corner for supporting a closet rod.

DECORATIVE BRACKET:
Wood or metal. Available in a huge range of styles and sizes. Most mount to walls with screws. Solid-wood versions may have recessed metal hangers along back edge for hiding screws.

STANDARDS & BRACKETS:
C-shaped, long pieces of strong metal, with many small vertical slots, that are mounted on a wall. Brackets, which come in various lengths from 4 to 18 inches for corresponding shelf depths, have hook-

shaped sections that lock into the slots on the standards. Heavy-duty versions have two columns of slots and corresponding double-hook brackets for added strength and stability.

PILASTERS & CLIPS:

Shallow, C-shaped light metal standards with horizontal slots that are installed in the sides of a cabinet or bookcase and hold small, V-shaped metal clips that snap into the vertical standards. Made in two versions: for surface mounting and for recessed mounting into channels cut into the cabinet sides.

SHELF PINS:

May be metal or plastic. Very small piece with a post on one side and flat support on the other; comes in various designs, including a rounded one called *spoon* type. Pins fit into predrilled ¼-inch holes in the sides of the cabinet or bookcase to support shelf ends.

USE TIPS:

Anchor shelf supports into wall studs whenever possible. Otherwise, use heavy-duty hollow-wall anchors, such as toggle bolts (page 34). Floating shelf brackets must be mounted to wall framing (studs or wood blocking).

BUYING TIPS:

For adjustable shelves, choose standards, pilasters, or shelf pins.

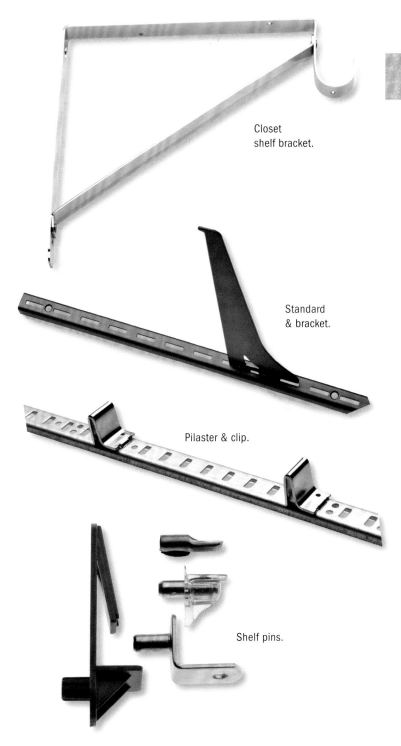

Closet shelf bracket.

Standard & bracket.

Pilaster & clip.

Shelf pins.

CHAPTER 5

SPECIALTY FASTENERS & SUPPORTS

Cotter Pin

DESCRIPTION:

Metal pin bent back upon itself, with slight open loop at the bend, similar to a hairpin. Generally only about 2 inches long, but available in smaller and larger sizes.

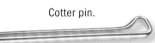

Cotter pin.

USE:

Generally used for holding metal rods or shafts, or to prevent slotted or castle nuts (page 32) from turning. The cotter pin is put through a tight hole and its tips are then bent to prevent it from sliding back out. The pin is removed by bending the tips straight again and pulling on the loop end with pliers.

USE TIP:

If you have to remove cotter pins repeatedly, get a small tool that looks like a hooked screwdriver, called a *cotter pin puller*.

Rivets & Similar Fasteners

DESCRIPTION & USE:

BLIND RIVET:

Commonly called a *POP® rivet*. A nail-like shaft fitted into a small, flanged, cylindrical head. The nail end is inserted into a rivet gun (a simple hand tool) and the head is inserted into a predrilled hole in the materials to be riveted. Squeezing the gun handles compresses the head, fastening the parts together, then cuts off the excess shaft. Available in *grip range* sizes corresponding to the thickness of the host materials. Used to fasten together pieces of light metal when there is access from one side only.

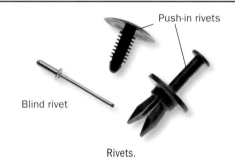

Push-in rivets

Blind rivet

Rivets.

PUSH-IN RIVET:

Plastic rivet with a broad, flat head and a barbed shaft. The shaft is inserted into a hole drilled in the material until the head is flush with the material. One version has a piston in the center of the head; after pushing in the shaft, you strike the piston with a hammer to secure the rivet. Used to join plastic automotive parts (such as bumper covers and underbelly pans) or to secure plastic or other thin paneling to walls and ceilings.

GROMMET:

Two ring-shaped parts that are pressed or driven together over the host material with grommet pliers or a hammer and grommet anvil. Anvils are commonly included in packages of grommets. Used to create a reinforced hole in tarps and other material, through which to thread rope.

T-nut

ALSO KNOWN AS:

Tee nut.

DESCRIPTION:

Metal fastener with a cylindrical barrel with internal threads and a flat cap with three sharp prongs. Barrel is inserted into predrilled hole in host material, then cap is hammered so prongs are driven into material until cap is flush with surface. A machine bolt is inserted through hole from other side of material and threaded into the T-nut.

USE:

Commonly used to anchor items to plywood and other wood sheet materials. T-nut stays in place, while bolt can be removed and reinstalled indefinitely.

T-nut.

Threaded Insert

DESCRIPTION:

Steel or brass cylinder with coarse wood-screw threads on its outside and machine-bolt threads on its inside. Insert is screwed into predrilled hole in wood with a large flat-head screwdriver. Bolt is threaded into insert to secure mating parts. A *barrel nut* is a similar fastener that is slip-fit into a hole rather then being threaded in.

USE:

Hidden connections on furniture, particularly modular, ready-to-assemble units or pieces with "knockdown" design that can be disassembled and reassembled.

Threaded insert.

Zip Tie

ALSO KNOWN AS:
Cable tie, plastic cable tie, nylon tie.

DESCRIPTION:
Small piece of plastic strap 4 inches or longer, one end of which has a small buckle that the other end is pulled through. Strap has a ribbed side that locks with the buckle. Conventional zip ties can only be tightened, never loosened, but there are also *releasable* or *reusable* versions. Disposable item; sold by the bagful.

USE:
One of the world's handiest fasteners. Far quicker than rope or string, neater than duct tape, and able to secure items very tightly. Also waterproof. Originally developed for binding cables together in electrical systems; can be applied to household tying tasks of all descriptions.

Zip ties.

USE TIPS:
CAUTION: Because these ties are easy to use and usually impossible to loosen, do not let unsupervised children play with them. Police and military personnel use heavy-duty zip ties as handcuffs.

BUYING TIPS:
Choose UV-resistant ties (typically colored black) for use in areas with sun exposure.

Turnbuckle

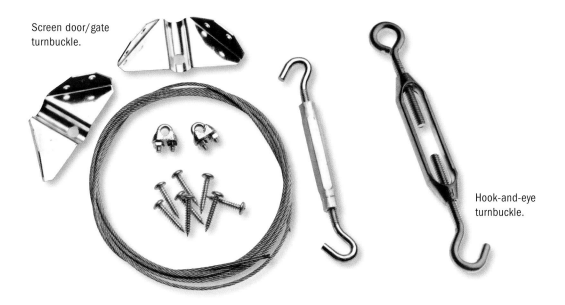

Screen door/gate turnbuckle.

Hook-and-eye turnbuckle.

DESCRIPTION:

An open, barrel-like metal device, internally threaded on both ends, with two threaded rods screwed in, one a left-handed thread, the other right-handed. The rods are usually less than a foot long, and may have an eye at both ends, a hook on one end and an eye on the other, or hooks on each end.

USE:

Acts as an adjustable segment of a cable or wire. The variations available allow flexibility of use: for instance, on one end, a cable could be attached to a hook while on the other a snap fastener and rope. A common use for a turnbuckle is to brace a screen door or a gate to prevent sagging.

USE TIPS:

The smaller sizes are zinc-plated, but the larger ones (all the way up to 2 feet) are galvanized.

BUYING TIPS:

Turnbuckles are sometimes sold in kits, such as for straightening out a screen door.

Braces & Plates

ALSO KNOWN AS:
Door and window braces.

DESCRIPTION:
All are flat metal, available in zinc- and brass-plated finishes.

INSIDE CORNER BRACE:
L-shaped piece with screw holes for mounting inside a corner. Comes in sizes 1 inch long and ½ inch wide to 8 inches long and 1 inch wide. Screw holes are staggered rather than being in a straight line. Specialty sources sell a thicker version excellent for chairs. Used for strengthening and supporting box and chair corners.

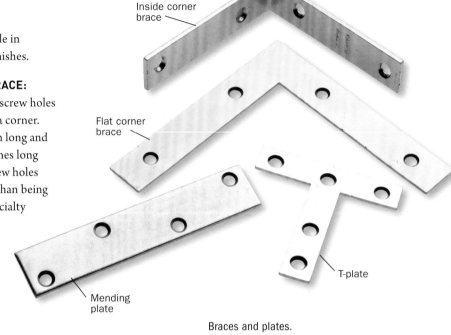

Braces and plates.

FLAT CORNER BRACE: L-shaped piece with screw holes for mounting on surface, at right angles to the corner brace version (above). A thicker, embossed version is specially made for screens. Used for bracing corners on window frames and doors.

MENDING PLATE:
Flat length of metal with screw holes. Used for joining two pieces of wood end-to-end, as well as many other applications—from reinforcing screen doors to strengthening furniture.

T-PLATE:
Flat metal piece made in the shape of the letter T; both horizontal and vertical legs of the T are the same length. Common use is for joining horizontal and vertical screen-door members.

Metal Angle

ALSO KNOWN AS:

Angle iron.

DESCRIPTION:

L-shaped steel or aluminum bar sold in a variety of sizes up to about 2 inches wide up to around ¼ inch thick, and sold by the foot. *Plain steel* angle has no holes; *slotted* angle has evenly spaced round and elongated holes along both sides; *punched* angle has round holes along both sides.

USES:

Punched and slotted angle are commonly used for bracing garage door tracks and automatic openers, and are handy for similar applications elsewhere around the house. Angle pieces are fastened to wood supports with lag screws or bolts and to one another with short bolts and nuts. Plain steel angle is useful for bracing or for creating a structural cleat or shelf edge on a wall. Requires drilling holes in fasteners, or pieces can be welded together, depending on the material.

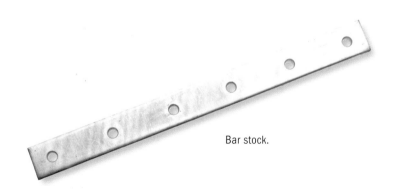

Slotted angle iron.

Bar Stock

DESCRIPTION:

Steel or aluminum flat bar commonly ⅛ or ¼ inches thick and 1 to 4 inches wide. May be *plain* (no holes) or *punched/ slotted* (with holes). Can be cut to length with a hacksaw and drilled for fastener holes. Some types can be welded together.

USE:

Commonly used for creating custom braces and supports.

Bar stock.

Metal Framing Channel

ALSO KNOWN AS:
Unistrut® (brand name).

DESCRIPTION:
Galvanized metal channel with an
overall square shape in cross section.
One face is open, creating the channel;
the opposing face is perforated with
elongated holes for fastening pieces
with bolts and nuts. Compatible with
a variety of fittings and brackets for
hanging or securing items from vertical
and horizontal surfaces.

Metal
framing channel.

USE:
Miscellaneous bracing and support, and
for structural assemblies, often in place of
lumber. Commonly used in commercial construction for hanging (via threaded rod; see page 30) electrical
conduit, plumbing pipe, and air ducts from ceilings.

CHAPTER 6

HINGES, HASPS & LATCHES

ABOUT HINGES

Hinges come in a tremendous array of styles and types, but there are some basics you can learn to help you make the best selection from the various models available.

Technically, hinges are "handed"—specified for use on left- or right-hand doors. But this can get complicated, and unless you're doing a special job you can forget it. Just flip the hinge over and it becomes left- or right-handed, as needed.

Hinges come in different sizes to support different weights. But this, too, can get complicated. To select the proper size, just determine if the hinge is in proportion, size-wise, to the door being hung and you'll be fine, even if you're undersized a bit—hinges are designed to be up to eight times stronger than they need to be.

Hinges also come in a variety of finishes and materials. Brass and plated brass are the most common, but there are many others, including stainless steel, galvanized steel, chrome-plated, and painted. Hinges also are designed for either surface-mounting or for recessing ("mortising") on the door and/or the frame. *Self-closing hinges* include *spring-loaded* hinges and *rising hinges* that are designed with an angular joint that uses gravity to close the door automatically.

Butt Hinge

DESCRIPTION:

Two rectangular metal plates, called "leaves," with screw holes and a pin joining the leaves. Each loop that holds the pin hole is called a "knuckle," and the knuckles and pin together are called the "barrel." Includes most standard door hinges and basic utility hinges.

USE:

Hanging interior and exterior house doors. Installing doors and other hinged parts on various projects.

BUYING TIPS:

Historically, a *butt* hinge has a non-removable pin that requires you to remove the door to take out the screws in one of the leaves; while a *loose-pin* hinge has

Butt hinge.

a removable pin that you can pull or tap out to remove the door. However, many butt hinges have removable pins, so if security is a concern, look for butt hinges with non-removable hinge pins.

Strap Hinge

DESCRIPTION:

Utility hinge with long, narrow leaves. Some strap hinges have two identical leaves; others have a rectangular leaf for the door frame and a strap-style leaf for the door; sometimes called a *T-hinge*. Ornamental versions have traditional or antique styling and attractive materials, such as hammered iron.

USE:

Utility projects where a rustic or industrial look is appropriate. Commonly used on outdoor projects, sheds, and storage boxes. Ornamental versions are available for all types of doors, including cabinet doors, house entry doors, barn doors, and gates.

BUYING TIPS:

Choose galvanized or stainless-steel hinges for outdoor use.

Strap hinges.

Gate Hinge

DESCRIPTION:

Heavy-duty outdoor hinges, often decorative, with one or two strap-style leaves. Installed with exterior wood screws, lag screws, or bolts. T-style gate hinges have a rectangular leaf that mounts to the door frame. Strap-style have two strap-style leaves. Pintle hinges have a lag-screw or bolt fitting with a large vertical pin (the pintle) that fastens to the gate post; a strap with a loop end fastens to the door and fits over the pintle.

Gate hinge.

Piano Hinge

ALSO KNOWN AS:

Continuous hinge.

DESCRIPTION:

Long, narrow hinge, commonly 1½ inches wide and up to
6 feet long, with screw holes every 2 inches.

USE:

Box and cabinet lids, furniture, and, of course, piano parts.
Hinge can be cut to length with a hacksaw. Offers a finished look
and precise motion with no side-to-side play.

BUYING TIPS:

Available in several finishes, including brass, nickel, stainless steel,
and chrome.

Piano hinge.

ABOUT CABINET HINGES

Cabinet hinges come in more types and styles than perhaps any other household hardware. To find the
right hinge for your application, you first have to consider how the door is installed. *Full-overlay* doors
completely overlap the frame around the cabinet opening. *Partial-inset*, or "lipped," doors have a recess
cut into their edges; the recessed portion fits inside the cabinet opening, while the lip overlaps the front
of the opening frame. *Inset*, or *flush*, doors fit inside the opening so their front faces are flush with the
cabinet front.

Next, consider how much of the hinge should be visible when the door is closed. *Concealed*
hinges are not visible. With a *semiconcealed* hinge, the barrel and some or all of the frame-side leaf are
exposed. An *exposed* or *surface-mount* hinge is installed on the front face of the door and frame and is
fully visible.

Then, there are the hinge styles, which can grouped very generally into two types: traditional hinges,
with two leaves and a pin, similar to a butt hinge (page 51); and European-style, which have a cupped
plate that is recessed into the door and is connected to the hinge body. The hinge body is clipped onto
a surface-mount plate on the cabinet. European-style hinges are commonly used on European-style
"frameless" cabinets, which have no face frame around the cabinet opening; but there are also many
varieties designed for traditional cabinets with face frames, called "framed." European-style hinges
typically are concealed and offer the great advantage of being fully adjustable, so you can fine-tune
each door's position after the doors are hung.

Cabinet Hinges

Semi-concealed hinge

DESCRIPTION:

SEMI-CONCEALED:
The historical standard. Used for overlay and partial-inset doors on framed cabinets.

EUROPEAN-STYLE:
The modern standard for kitchen cabinets. Concealed hinges, typically with multiple adjustment features. Various types and styles available for framed and frameless cabinets.

SURFACE-MOUNT:
Hinge with two flat, decorative leaves, similar to a butt hinge (page 51). Typically traditional or antique styling but also available for contemporary and retro-modern looks. Usually require framed cabinets with inset doors.

PIVOT:
Mounted on or near top and bottom of door. Hinged on a pivot mechanism rather than a pin. Concealed and semi-concealed versions available, with types for overlay, partial-inset, and inset doors.

European-style hinge

Surface-mount hinge

BUYING TIPS:
When replacing old hinges, it's best to bring a set of the original hinges to the store for comparison to make sure you get the correct style and size. Cabinet door and drawer knobs and pulls are available in styles and finishes to match hinges.

Hasps

Hasp (safety style)

DESCRIPTION:
Hasps may be plain or decorative, with the length of the slotted part ranging from 2 ¼ to 6 ¼ inches, with staples (the part with the ring for the lock) of proportionate sizes and hasp widths 1 to 2 inches. Some models may have a key lock instead of a ring.

A *safety hasp* has a slotted part that conceals the screws, securing the hasp when it is closed. Some safety hasps are heavy-duty and have a square hole for insertion of a $5/16$-inch carriage bolt.

Another type of hasp is designed for use on chests and sliding doors. Here, the end is upturned and also hides the mounting screws.

Decorative hasps are available with bright brass finishes.

USE:
Securing doors, usually outdoor types, with a padlock that goes through the ring.

Latches

BASIC TYPES:
Sliding, or barrel, bolt
Hook-and-eye latch
Cane bolt

DESCRIPTION & USE:
Devices that keep gates and doors closed but typically not locked. They can also block gates open. Generally consists of a horizontal piece attached to a gate or door that either slides, falls, or snaps into a catch on the doorframe or gate post. Many different types and styles, including:

SLIDING, OR BARREL, BOLT:
Long bolt with handle projecting from middle slides in and out of curved piece on door frame. Available in lightweight versions for decorative purposes and in extreme heavyweight versions, sometimes called *square spring bolts* or *night latches*, for security purposes, such as on the insides of exterior doors. Larger bolts come with a hole in the bolt so that they can be padlocked.

HOOK-AND-EYE LATCH:
Also called *gate hook*. Consists of a screw eye that screws into a gate post or door frame and a corresponding screw eye and hook that is secured to the gate or door. Common sizes are 1 to 5 inches long but can be up to 18 inches long. A "safety" version is available with a spring-loaded bolt that snaps across the hook opening to keep small children from unhooking the gate.

CANE BOLT:
L-shaped bolt that slides through two mounting brackets. Installed vertically to use gravity action. Typically used to secure one of the double doors on a shed or barn.

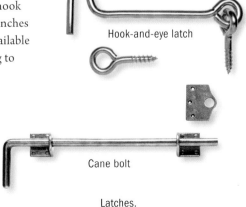

Sliding bolt

Hook-and-eye latch

Cane bolt

Latches.

CHAPTER 7

CHAIN & CABLE

ABOUT CHAIN

Chain comes in around forty different varieties, but most of your needs will be filled by the small selection commonly available in stores, as described here. Sections are usually cut to your order from reels, though some decorative chain comes packaged. Size denominations vary from type to type, so study the label on the reel or package for important technical information.

Chain may be put into two groups: chain whose primary purpose is strength, and chain whose main purpose is decoration. Whatever type you buy, however, check to make sure it's strong enough for the job at hand. All chain is classified and marked according to its *working load limit*, meaning how much stress may be applied before the chain snaps. Most are specifically marked "not for overhead lifting."

Load limits vary according to the thickness of the chain and the metal it's made of. So, for example, #10 (1-inch-long links) brass jack chain, which is decorative, has a working load limit of 34 pounds. But grade 30-proof coil chain in about the same size, but made of steel, has a load limit of 800 pounds. And a cam-alloy version has a limit of 5,100 pounds in the same size. Check the label of the chain container or the manufacturer's catalog for the chain's working load limit.

In addition to the specific chains detailed below, which are mainly available from reels, there are packaged chains designed for specific purposes, such as dog runners, hanging porch swings, and various vehicular jobs. Chain also comes in pails, boxes, drums, and bags.

For safety, you should observe the following:

- Follow load limits on a chain—don't overload it. Dealers can supply load limits from charts they have. However, it is okay to load it right up to its limit.
- Don't use a chain for overhead lifting unless it is specified for that use.
- Don't apply tension if a chain is twisted.
- Pull a chain gradually from an at-rest position—don't jerk it.
- Don't use a chain that looks damaged.

Bead Chain

DESCRIPTION:

Hollow, round metal beads joined by dumbbell-shaped connectors. Beads may also be elliptically shaped. Comes in chrome-, brass-, and nickel-plated finishes.

USE:

Used for decorative purposes around the home and as lamp pulls.

USE TIPS:

The main advantage of bead chain is that it will not kink or tangle. You can twist it every which way and it will fall out straight.

BUYING TIPS:

At local stores you are likely to get only a couple of sizes of bead chain, plus packaged chain for lamp pulls. Hardware stores carry catalogs that list manufacturers from whom you can get a much wider selection. You can buy connectors separately, such as when you want to lengthen a bead chain.

Bead chain.

Decorative Chain

ALSO KNOWN AS:

Decor chain.

Decorative chain.

DESCRIPTION:

Lightweight chain available in a variety of handsome finishes, including brass and colors—antique white, antique copper, and black. Loops are generally large ovals of wire.

USE:

Hanging lamps, plants, and for hanging on draperies and other decorative effects.

Double-Loop Chain

ALSO KNOWN AS:
Weldless, non-welded, Inco (brand name), Tenso (brand name).

DESCRIPTION:
Lightweight steel links that are knotted into long double loops for linkage instead of being welded. Sizes run from No. 5 (smallest) though 0 to 8/0 (largest). A *single-loop*, or *lock link*, version is available, primarily for use in machinery.

USE:
Household jobs from decoration to shelf supports. Among the strongest of the decorative chains. Heavier sizes—over 1/0—can be used to hang hammocks and some playground equipment.

Double-loop chain.

Proof Coil Chain

DESCRIPTION:
Strongest steel chain, with welded, slightly oblong links. Available in galvanized, plain steel, and zinc finishes. Comes in four grades: Grade 30 (most common), 40, 70 ("high test"), and 80 (made of alloy steel, with the highest load limits—up to 80,000 pounds). The $\frac{5}{16}$-inch size Grade 30 has a working load limit of 1,900 pounds. The fractional sizes refer to the diameter of the steel.

USE:
Very heavy pulling jobs where motorized equipment is involved, such as in agriculture or for towing cars.

Proof coil chain.

Jack Chain

DESCRIPTION:
A strong decorative chain of varying load limits made of twisted figure-eight links. Comes in hot-galvanized, brass-plated, bright zinc, and solid brass; and in single and double versions.

USES:
Often used for functions where decoration and light support are needed, such as for hanging large plants, signs, and children's toys.

Jack chain.

Welded General-Use Chain

TYPES:
Coil chain
Machine chain
Passing link chain

Straight-link
machine chain.

DESCRIPTION & USE:
Similar to but not as strong as proof coil chain (page 58). Material is less than ¼ inch thick. Sizes are measured in gauges, from No. 4 (smallest— inside of links about ½ inch long) through 3, 2, 1, and on to 1/0 to 5/0 (largest—inside of links about 1 inch long). Commonly used on agricultural implements, tailgates, overhead doors, for security purposes, or general utility.

COIL:
Longest link of these three. Available in straight-link and twist-link styles.

MACHINE:
Slightly shorter links. Also available in straight-link and twist-link styles.

PASSING LINK:
Slightly rounded links that prevent binding and kinking.

Safety Chain

ALSO KNOWN AS:
Plumber's chain.

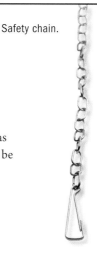

Safety chain.

DESCRIPTION:
Flat, stamped brass chain of oval links that resist entanglement.

USE:
Used by plumbers in toilet tanks (as link between flush lever and flapper) and as a general utility chain. It is available in bright zinc and solid brass and may also be used for decorative purposes.

Sash Chain

ALSO KNOWN AS:
Weldless flat chain.

DESCRIPTION:
Flat, teardrop-shaped stamped links that appear folded over one another.

USE:
Good replacement material for sash cords on double-hung windows, as it rides over window pulleys easily; also for tub and basin stoppers.

BUYING TIPS:
Sash chain comes in plain metal and bronze, but if you live in an area where sea air is present, sash chain is inadvisable—it can rust out.

Sash chain

Plastic Chain

DESCRIPTION:
Available in a variety of colors and shapes.

USE:
Strictly decorative and non–weight-bearing jobs. Plastic chain offers no reliable load rating and can easily develop hidden cracks or become brittle.

Plastic chain.

Chain Connectors

TYPES:
S-hook
Clevis slip hook
Clevis grab hook
Lap link
Quick link
Mechanical connecting link
Cold shut

Cold shut

Clevis grab hook

S-hook

Lap link

Quick link

Chain connectors.

DESCRIPTION:

S-HOOK:
Open-ended metal link shaped like the letter S. Small, lightweight versions can be crimped shut with pliers after being hooked onto chain. Stronger types should not be bent or closed. Because S-hooks don't close, they are suitable only for downward forces, and they are not designed for anything that requires a high degree of safety, such as swings and other play equipment.

CLEVIS SLIP HOOK:
Looks like a hefty fishhook. Used for looping chain and hooking it back onto itself to create a loop of any size. The clevis (pin) end of the slip hook is secured to the end of the chain, while the chain is slipped through the hook to form the lasso loop.

CLEVIS GRAB HOOK:
Shaped like a clevis slip hook, but is narrower. Works like a clevis slip hook, but its narrowness allows it to lock onto one link.

LAP LINK:
Also called *repair link*. Partially open link that looks like it has almost been cut in half sidewise. Can be used wherever life or limb does not depend on link's integrity to link two sections of any chain together. Lap link is hooked onto chain links, then squeezed closed with pliers. Commonly used with tire chains.

QUICK LINK:
Link with a gap on one side that has a coupling nut on one end and threads on the other. Nut is tightened with a wrench after chains are connected. The closed connection makes quick links more secure than S-hooks and stronger than spring-loaded connectors, such as carabiners. However, they should not be used as permanent connectors, because the nut can potentially loosen by itself and therefore should be checked periodically.

MECHANICAL CONNECTING LINK:
Also called *coupling link*. Two U-shaped link halves joined by a metal pin system activated with a hammer. For heavy-duty permanent or semipermanent connections.

COLD SHUT:
Open-ended link device that is hammered shut after connecting chain sections. Designed for permanent connections (they cannot be reused after being shut once), but loading is questionable because link can reopen or not close completely, and because bending metal always weakens it.

BUYING TIPS:
All chain connectors should have an equal or greater load rating than the chain(s) which with they are used.

Cable

DESCRIPTION:

What most of us call "cable" (as in strong metal cable, not cable-TV cable), the hardware industry typically calls "wire rope." Technically speaking, *cable* often refers to stranded metal wire or rope that is up to ⅜ inch in diameter, while *wire rope* is greater than ⅜ inch, but this terminology is used inconsistently. In any case, if a hardware supplier sells wire rope, it is stranded metal cable—the same thing.

Vinyl-coated cable.

Stainless steel cable.

Galvanized cable.

Cable commonly sold in stores ranges in size from ⅛ to ⅜ inches in diameter and in spooled lengths up to about 200 feet. Choose a cable with a load rating—or *breaking strength*—suitable for your purpose. If corrosion-resistance is important, choose 302 or 304 stainless-steel cable. Galvanized cable offers some corrosion-resistance but will rust if its zinc coating is breached. As with chain, cable is only as strong as its connections, so be sure to use appropriately rated clamps and other fittings (page 63) and install them as directed by the manufacturer.

NOTE:

Cable sold by hardware suppliers typically is not strong enough for zip lines or overhead loads. Zip lines are made with high-strength aircraft cable, and even a small backyard setup should have cable with a load rating of 7,000 pounds or more.

USE:

Dog runs, guy wires for anchoring trees and fences, clothesline, general tie-down applications. Cable does not stretch and is generally stronger than rope and easier to use than chain. Vinyl-coated cable is popular for dog runs and clotheslines because it's cleaner and more visible than standard uncoated cable. Coated cable may or may not be galvanized; galvanized is better because it's less likely to rust when the vinyl coating (inevitably) becomes damaged.

USE TIPS:

Always use cable clamps (page 63) for securing cable ends and thimbles (page 63) for making loops in cable. Tying cable into knots or using unsuitable hardware significantly decreases its strength and corrosion-resistance.

Cable Fittings

DESCRIPTION & USE:

CLAMP:

U-shaped bolt with a clamping *saddle* and two nuts. Secures two sections of cable when making a loop in a single cable or splicing two cables together (requires multiple clamps).

FERRULE

Also called *sleeve*. Metal sleeve designed for crimping onto one or two cables (or two sections of same cable) to create loops or splices. Alternative to a cable clamp. Requires a swaging tool to properly crimp.

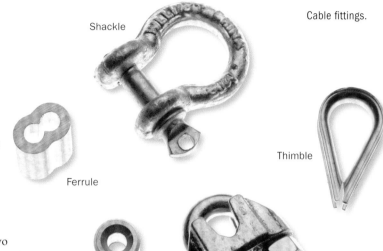

Shackle

Cable fittings.

Thimble

Ferrule

Stop

Clamp

STOP:

Metal ring used to crimp around cable end to prevent cable from slipping through a hole or fitting and to prevent unraveling. A swaging tool is required for proper crimping.

THIMBLE:

Teardrop-shaped metal sleeve for forming a loop in cable. Cable is wrapped around outside of thimble, then clamped tightly at pointed end of thimble. Protects cable from abrasion and wear, and prevents kinking, which decreases strength.

SHACKLE:

Horseshoe-shaped metal fitting with threaded bolt at open end of horseshoe. Used to secure cable to an eye bolt or other anchor point. Shackle connects to cable via a loop created with a thimble.

CHAPTER 8

WIRE & WIRE PRODUCTS

Wire

DESCRIPTION:

May be *single-strand drawn wire* or *twisted strand*; the first is a single piece of wire, the latter three or four strands twisted together. Both types come galvanized for outdoor use (short lengths are available in copper and aluminum, too) and both may be had in various gauges, from about 10 gauge to 24 gauge. Picture-hanging wire comes in stainless steel and even nylon, sometimes called "invisible." Heavy metal wire may be categorized as *cable* or *wire rope* (page 62). Very thin wire may be called *hobby wire* or *flower wire*. *Picture wire* is woven cable of medium strength.

USE:

General-purpose wire is useful for any number of tasks, from binding other materials to mending fences. In the very light gauges—18 and 20—wire can be used for hanging pictures or tying Christmas wreaths. Tie-wire for rebar is an inexpensive steel wire that's handy for quick fastening, bundling branches, and other temporary jobs; it bends, twists, and cuts easily but also breaks easily if twisted too much.

Hardware Cloth

ALSO KNOWN AS:

Wire mesh.

DESCRIPTION:

Galvanized metal screening made of wire welded into a grid. Relatively flexible, it comes in rolls of widths ranging from 24 to 36 or 48 inches, and in 19- and 23-gauge wire; 19-gauge is heavier and stronger. Mesh size—the size of the squares in the wire grid—is typically ¼ or ½ inch.

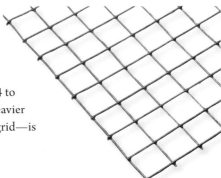

USE:

Various: as a sifter of sand and topsoil; a pet cage material; as a fence wherever you want extra security. It is frequently used to keep birds, bats, and squirrels out of houses and rabbits and deer out of gardens.

USE TIPS:

Much better than chicken wire for animal containment/control, due to smaller openings and stronger wire. You can cut hardware cloth quite easily with tin snips or aviation snips.

Poultry Netting

ALSO KNOWN AS:

Chicken wire, hexagonal netting.

DESCRIPTION:

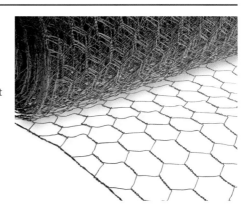

Galvanized wire woven—not welded—into a netting that has large squares or hexagons—1 or 2 inches wide—and comes in various heights up to 6 feet and lengths of 50 to 150 feet. The wire is of a lighter gauge than hardware cloth (page 64). Some brands have horizontal lines of wire through the lower hexagons to make a tighter mesh.

USE:

Protection against encroachment of small animals on property; for example, installation on a split-rail fence as a way to keep a dog confined.

BUYING TIPS:

Though not as strong as hardware cloth, netting is very inexpensive and can serve well for many jobs. Ironically, chicken wire is not recommended for protecting chickens from predators; coyotes and other animals can tear through the material, and rats can fit through the openings in standard chicken wire.

Welded Wire Fencing

ALSO KNOWN AS:

Horse fence, garden fence, rabbit netting.

DESCRIPTION:

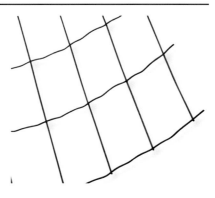

Galvanized wire mesh welded into rectangular grid pattern. Sold in rolls 25 to 200 feet long and heights from 24 to 72 inches. Wire gauges include 12, 14, and 16, with 12 being the heaviest. Mesh sizes (rectangular openings) range from $1/2$ to 2 inches wide and 1 to 4 inches tall. Vinyl-coated versions available in green and black.

USE:

Permanent or temporary infill material between wood or metal fence posts, commonly used for animal enclosures. Handy for temporary fencing to protect trees and garden areas from animals.

USE TIPS:

Attaches to wood supports with U-shaped nails (also called poultry staples) and to metal supports with galvanized wire. Cut fencing with heavy-duty wire cutters or linesman pliers.

PART II
GENERAL MATERIALS

CHAPTER 9

ADHESIVES, CAULKS & SEALANTS

Some of the adhesives useful in home carpentry include carpenter's wood glue, exterior carpenter's glue, liquid hide glue, polyurethane glue, panel adhesive, latex caulk, silicone caulk, and a hot glue gun with glue sticks.

Wood Glue

ALSO KNOWN AS:
Woodworker's glue, yellow glue, carpenter's glue, aliphatic glue, aliphatic resin glue.

DESCRIPTION:
Classic wood glue is similar to household white glue but is yellowish and slightly thicker. It's still the best option for wood-to-wood joints that fit snugly. It dries relatively quickly and cleans up with water. Available in standard (for indoor projects) and waterproof (for indoor or outdoor projects) formulas.

USE TIPS:
When properly applied to clean wood joints, the bond typically is stronger than the wood itself. However, wood glue does not fill gaps in joints, so if there's any looseness in the joint or play between the mating parts, use polyurethane glue (page 69) instead.

Polyurethane Glue

ALSO KNOWN AS:
Gorilla Glue® (brand name), all-purpose glue.

DESCRIPTION:
The Superman of household adhesives. Thick, super-sticky, brownish liquid glue sold in small squeeze bottles. Bonds to wood, metal, plastic, stone, foam, glass, ceramic, masonry, and more. Waterproof. Not affected by hot or cold temperatures. Expands as it cures, making it great for tightening up loose-fitting joints, such as those on rickety chair legs.

USE TIPS:
Follow the manufacturer's application instructions carefully. This moisture-cured glue requires moistening of one of the mating parts to activate the curing process. Also somewhat messy, nearly impossible to clean from unwanted surfaces, and stains anything it touches, including your hands (the brownish stains have to wear off over a few days). Don't apply too much because the glue foams up during curing, expanding to three times its original volume.

Super Glue

ALSO KNOWN AS:
Instant glue, Krazy Glue® (brand name).

DESCRIPTION:
Thin, clear liquid glue sold in tiny tubes and squeeze bottles. Technically known as *cyanoacrylate adhesive*. The classic choice for repairing broken coffee cups and other non-porous materials, as well as just about anything else it'll stick to.

USE TIPS:
Apply sparingly; often won't stick if too much is applied. Requires a tight-fitting joint; won't fill even small gaps. Works best if you can hold the mating pieces together for 30 to 60 seconds while the glue sets. *Warning: Sticks extremely well to skin!*

Epoxy

DESCRIPTION:
Two-part, all-purpose adhesive consisting of a catalyst and hardener that are mixed prior to application. Bonds to virtually everything. Sold in double-barreled syringes that do the mixing for you or in small tubes for mixing yourself. When you have a job that you can't imagine a glue doing, think epoxy.

USE TIPS:

Epoxy dries to a very hard, typically clear, plastic. It sticks to more materials than super glue (page 69) and is excellent at filling gaps, so it's often used like a heavy-duty super glue. It's also thicker than super glue and therefore more visible when dried.

BUYING TIPS:

Epoxy syringes are handy and less messy than tubes, but tubes typically last longer in storage because syringes tend to dry or cure at the tips. Most epoxies do a similar job, but some are harder and/or more heat-tolerant than others. The strongest typically are sold in tubes.

Construction Adhesive

ALSO KNOWN AS:

Liquid Nails® (brand name), construction glue.

DESCRIPTION:

Goopy, tan-colored adhesive sold in large tubes (for applying with a caulking gun) and smaller squeeze tubes. Very strong, general-purpose adhesive for heavy-duty construction joints.

USE:

Commonly used to bond wood to wood or wood to masonry, such as wall framing to concrete slabs or foundation walls. Also excellent for bonding brick, concrete block, stone, and other masonry materials. Waterproof for outdoor projects.

Contact Cement

DESCRIPTION:

Mid-weight, sticky adhesive sold in paint-style cans. Applied to large, flat, smooth surfaces with a foam roller (small paint roller). Must be applied comprehensively to both mating surfaces and allowed to become tacky or dry to the touch before the surfaces are bonded together. Forms an extremely strong bond that remains somewhat flexible over time.

USE:

Most often used to bond plastic laminate (such as Formica®) to particleboard and other materials for countertops and cabinets. Similarly useful for bonding other sheet materials to flat surfaces.

USE TIPS:

When you apply contact adhesive to one of the mating materials and let it dry to the touch, the glue itself isn't very sticky, but once it touches the cement on the other glued surface it forms an instant, very strong bond that gets stronger when pressure is applied. Make sure your mating pieces are properly aligned before letting the glued surfaces touch. Once joined, press the pieces together with a hard-rubber roller (called a J-roller or laminate roller) or similar tool. Heavy fumes; use in well-ventilated areas.

Thread-Lock Adhesive

ALSO KNOWN AS:
Thread-locker, thread sealant, Loctite® (brand name), anaerobic adhesive.

DESCRIPTION:
One-part adhesive that cures without air. Seals nuts and bolt threads to prevent them from loosing due to vibration.

USE:
When you really don't want a nut or bolt coming loose and it's not designed for a cotter pin (page 44), squirt a little thread-locker onto the threads. Forms a hard plastic that stays on the metal parts but can be broken when you loosen the parts with a wrench or other tool. Can replace or be used with lock washers, setscrews, locking nuts, etc.

Caulk

ABOUT CAULK (& SEALANT):
Don't make the common mistake of assuming all caulks are more or less the same. In reality, caulk (and caulk-like sealants) is as diverse as tape. You wouldn't use Scotch tape on your ductwork, just as you shouldn't use painter's caulk for your plumbing fixtures. Caulk manufacturers tend to exaggerate the suitable applications of their products, so don't rely on the product labels alone. It's better to focus on the caulk material and narrow down your options from there. Caulks that are called "sealants" typically are designed for outdoor applications, such as windows and doors, siding, and roofing.

DESCRIPTION:
Elastomeric (flexible) and adhesive goo of various materials and colors most often sold in 6-ounce squeeze tubes or 10- to 11-ounce, 8-inch-long cartridges for applying with a caulking gun. Used to seal gaps, joints, and seams in a range of materials, for appearance and/or to protect against moisture. May or may not be paintable; may or may not be mildew resistant; more or less flexible or adhesive depending on formulation and quality.

USE:
Different caulks and sealants are designed for different applications. Here are the basic material categories, their characteristics, and common uses:

ACRYLIC OR VINYL LATEX CAULK:
Generally, water-based caulks (as opposed to silicone or rubber caulks, below). Standard "painter's caulk," commonly used for interior materials such as trimwork, cabinets, wall and ceiling corners, and other areas that usually get painted. Easy to apply and cleans up with water. Dries quickly. Formulations with silicone offer improved durability and flexibility over standard versions but should not be used in place of true silicone caulk. Good for interior work, but generally not durable in outdoor applications, despite manufacturer claims.

SILICONE CAULK:

Pure (100 percent) silicone caulk remains the standard for sinks, faucets, ceramic tile, countertops, tubs, showers, and other indoor areas where long-term water resistance is critical. It's messier, smellier, and harder to apply than latex caulk, but it holds up much better in wet conditions and remains flexible for far longer. For kitchens and bathrooms, choose mildew- and bacteria-resistant formulas to protect against damage and staining from mold and mildew. Silicone works well in cold and hot temperatures and adheres best to nonporous surfaces, such as metal, glass, and ceramic. It does not bond well to wood. When applying to metal, choose a "neutral-cure" formula, which bonds better and is less likely to corrode some metals than standard "acid-cure" silicone that contains acetoxy and has a vinegar-like odor.

POLYURETHANE SEALANT:

High-performance exterior caulk for sealing wood, metal, and masonry joints. More flexible and durable than latex/acrylic and other standard "exterior" caulk formulas. Unlike pure silicone, urethane sealants often are paintable. Expensive, but worth it for critical applications, such as doors and windows and metal roof flashing.

RUBBER CAULK:

Exterior caulk made with butyl or other synthetic rubber compounds. Goopy, messy, but ultra water-resistant. Good for patching gutters and metal roofing and flashing. Not compatible with some roofing materials, such as modified-bitumen flashing tape and rubberized asphalt flashing and roof membranes.

BUYING TIPS:

Splurge for the good stuff and avoid the cheap stuff, especially for outdoor projects. A few extra bucks for a tube of good caulk can prevent hundreds or thousands of dollars of damage to the materials it's protecting.

Spray Foam Insulation

DESCRIPTION:

High-tech foam insulation in an aerosol can. Comes with a straw-like applicator tip that allows you to spray the foam into narrow crevices and cracks. The foam is incredibly sticky and expands to fill cavities. Dries to a hard or semi-flexible state, depending on the type. Different formulas have different expansion rates. High-expanding versions grow to many times their applied volume. Low-expanding and non-expanding

Spray foam insulation.

foams grow only a little and do so with less force to prevent bowing of door and window jambs, among other problems caused by excessive expansion.

USE:

Air-sealing and insulating around door and window frames; wall, ceiling, and roof penetrations; foundation walls; light fixtures; etc. It's not pretty, so use it only where looks aren't important or where it will be hidden by finish materials. For example, to seal around door and window frames, you remove the interior casing (trim molding) and spray the foam between the structural wall framing and the door/window jambs. Using spray foam is much more effective for sealing and insulating than the old familiar technique of cramming fiberglass insulation into small cavities.

USE TIPS:

Apply carefully and beware of expansion! Spray foam does an excellent job sticking to everything in its path, including clothes, skin, wood—everything. All spray foams expand, including non-expanding types, so use sparingly—especially when you first use, until you know how much the foam will grow.

Blacktop Sealer

ALSO KNOWN AS:

Driveway sealer.

DESCRIPTION:

Heavy black liquid with coal tar or neoprene base. Ordinarily comes in five-gallon cans but also available in smaller containers as a *crack patcher*.

USE:

To renew the appearance of asphalt driveways and to provide a waterproof coating that also protects against oil and other staining materials. Also for sealing small cracks.

USE TIPS:

Blacktop sealer can be applied with a brush, roller, or push broom. Using a roller on a stick or a push broom makes the job easier.

BUYING TIPS:

Blacktop sealer can vary in quality greatly; poor-quality material can be as thin as water. The thicker the material, the better.

Blacktop Patcher

ALSO KNOWN AS:
Asphalt patch, cold patcher, cold-mix asphalt.

DESCRIPTION:
Chunky black material with the consistency of very soft tar. Comes ready to use in various-sized bags or plastic buckets.

USE:
Repair large cracks and holes in asphalt driveways; used to pave small walks.

USE TIPS:
Blacktop patcher is poured in place and then tamped to a solid density. Driving a car back and forth over a small patch is one good way to compress it, or use a heavy lawn roller.

Roofing Cements

TYPES:
Asphalt plastic roof cement
Damp patch roof cement
Lap/double-coverage roof cement
Quick-setting asphalt roof cement

ALSO KNOWN AS:
Mastic.

DESCRIPTION:
All of these roofing cements contain petroleum solvents; use outdoors only.

> **ASPHALT PLASTIC CEMENT:**
> Fairly viscous black goo of asphalt and mineral fibers. Comes in two grades: regular, and flashing, which is thicker. Adheres to any dry surface.

Like most cements, comes in one- and five-gallon cans. However, some similar products are available in standard 10.5-ounce caulking cartridges for application with a caulking gun. The standard material for sealing edges of flashing and patches in flat roofs, as well as installation of the bottom layers of roll roofing. Also for repairing leaks in gutters. Applied with a trowel over reinforcement fabric or roofing tape—a 4- to 6-inch-wide, loosely woven glass fiber or cotton mesh membrane, sold in long rolls.

DAMP PATCH CEMENT (ALSO KNOWN AS *WET OR DRY ROOF CEMENT*):

Similar to the above but specially formulated to adhere to wet surfaces. Used for emergency repairs under extreme dampness, such as leaks under snow buildup or during a major rainstorm. Applied with a trowel.

LAP CEMENT:

Thick black adhesive, similar to the above cement but thinner. Used to seal overlapping strips of roll roofing or shingle tabs. Applied with a brush or roller.

QUICK-SETTING ASPHALT CEMENT:

As the name implies, this sets very quickly. Basically an asphalt plastic cement with more solvent in it. Comes in various consistencies from fluid to thick. Used to adhere strip shingles in windy areas.

USE TIPS:

Patching over and over again may indicate a more serious problem that needs to be solved by a new roof or an overall coating with a material called *roof coating*, or *asphalt roof paint*, which is applied with a big brush. This will fill small gaps. Roof coating, also called *foundation coating*, is a masonry waterproofer. Both can extend the life of a flat roof.

CHAPTER 10

METAL & PLASTIC SHEETING

Sheet Metal

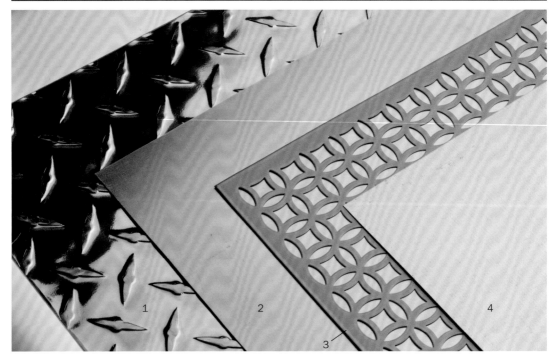

1. Diamond plate; 2. galvanized steel; 3. perforated aluminum; 4. plain aluminum.

TYPES:
Diamond plate
Galvanized steel sheet
Aluminum sheet, perforated
Aluminum sheet, plain

DESCRIPTION & USE:
Thin metal (typically less than ¹⁄₁₆ inch thick) that is easily bent and cut without special equipment other than tin snips.

DIAMOND PLATE:
Aluminum or galvanized steel sheet covered on one side with crisscrossed diamond pattern, creating a textured surface that is somewhat decorative and slip-resistant. Heavier-duty than standard sheet metals. Used for a variety of applications, such as door kickplates, high-traffic floor areas, and loading ramps.

GALVANIZED STEEL:

Standard sheet metal, sometimes called "tin." Sold in sheets of various sizes and in rolls commonly 2 feet wide and 8 feet long. Used for a variety of repair and hole-patching jobs.

ALUMINUM SHEET, PERFORATED:

Sold in 3 × 3-foot squares and 3 × 8-foot sheets in various perforations. Available also in anodized finishes, such as gold, and many different patterns. Sometimes called radiator grill, after its main use of concealing old-fashioned radiators.

ALUMINUM SHEET, PLAIN:

Most often sold in 2 × 3-foot and 3 × 3-foot squares. Used for lining walls next to stoves, hobby projects, etc.

BUYING TIPS:

Thin, plain sheet metal is often stocked with HVAC (heating, ventilation, and air conditioning) parts and equipment, because that's what most air ducting is made from.

Rigid Plastic Sheet

ALSO KNOWN AS:

Plexiglas®, Lucite® (brand names), Lexan™, acrylic sheet, plastic glazing.

DESCRIPTION:

The most common rigid plastic is acrylic; it comes clear or in textures and colors. Sold in a range of sizes that you can cut to size as needed. Common thicknesses are about ⅛ and ¼ inches. Plexiglas® and Lucite® are acrylic. Lexan™ is polycarbonate, which is much stronger than acrylic (also more expensive); use it when strength
is important.

USE:

Extremely versatile product used in an infinite array of decorative and functional projects, including art, hobbies, small shelves, and repairs—and to replace glass window panes.

USE TIPS:

Can be bent by heating slightly, drilled at slow speed, cut with a variety of tools, as well as glued (in some cases) and sanded on the edges (not the surfaces). Cuts easily with a circular saw, jigsaw, or hacksaw but should be well supported to prevent cracking the brittle material. Also can be scored and snapped with a utility knife or a special tool called a *plastic cutter*. Just score it several times along a line and then break it off. When drilling holes, support it directly underneath the hole with a block of wood. Leave the protective paper on both sides of the material until you're ready to install it or put it to use. Plastic sheeting scratches very easily (especially acrylic) and cannot be repaired.

Roof Flashing

TYPES:

Step flashing
Flat flashing
Roll flashing
Pipe/vent flashing

DESCRIPTION & USE:

Sheet metal pieces for roof repairs and installations. May be copper .01 inches thick or more, but aluminum and galvanized steel are much more common. Sold in a wide variety of shapes and sizes. Standard types for roof repairs include:

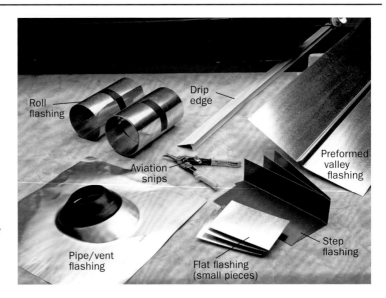

STEP FLASHING:

L-shaped pieces about 7 inches long and 4 inches wide on each side of the L. Designed to be layered into shingle courses going up a sloped roof. Commonly used along chimneys and where a sloped roof abuts a wall.

FLAT FLASHING:

Flat sheet metal that can be cut and bent as needed. Used as an all-purpose flashing material.

ROLL FLASHING:

Also called *valley flashing* (and sometimes "w" flashing, due to it's shape). Thin, flat metal sold in rolls from 6 to 20 inches wide and lengths up to 50 feet. Used to create a runoff channel where two sloping roof planes meet. Valleys typically are replaced only during roof replacement, but the rolls are handy for other flashing job and miscellaneous roof repairs.

PIPE/VENT FLASHING:

Flat metal base with a raised dome (or other shape) near the center. The dome has a hole and is covered with, or made of, rubber to seal around plumbing pipes and other materials that penetrate up through roofing.

NOTE:

Flashing is also a verb and may refer to the use of roof cement/sealant products around chimneys, skylights, and edges of roofs.

USE TIPS:

Make sure that the flashing used is compatible with the roofing. For example, don't use copper with red cedar shakes, because copper will darken the cedar. Be sure to seal flashing at the edges with roofing cement or sealant. Cut flashing with aviation snips or similar shears made for thin metals.

Plastic Sheeting

ALSO KNOWN AS:

Polyethylene sheeting, Visqueen (brand name).

DESCRIPTION:

All-purpose plastic sheet available in roll form and in various thicknesses—2-mil, 4-mil, 6-mil, etc.— and a wide range of widths and lengths. Note that "mil" is a unit of measure equal to 1/1,000 of an inch (0.001 inches); it is not an abbreviation for "millimeter." The standard thickness for many construction jobs is 6-mil. Sold in clear and black.

USE:

Many different uses, but chiefly as covers and drop cloths. Used in construction projects for moisture barriers under concrete slabs and vapor barriers in insulated walls and ceilings.

USE TIPS:

Do not use thin plastic sheeting on floors—it is extremely slippery.

BUYING TIPS:

If you are using plastic as a drop cloth, make sure you get 6-mil or thicker material. The thinnest ones available tear very easily, making them worthless for that purpose (and they are generally hard to use).

Window Film

ALSO KNOWN AS:

Window kit, shrink film kit, window insulator.

DESCRIPTION:

Ultra-thin, clear plastic sheeting that shrinks when heat is applied with a hair dryer. Commonly sold in kits containing the plastic film and double-sided tape. Also available in bulk rolls of film, which is more cost-effective when you have a lot of windows to seal.

USE:

Sealing over drafty windows in winter. To apply window film, you cut a piece a little bit larger than the window opening and apply it to the trim frame around the window with double-sided tape. Then, you heat the film with a hair dryer, causing it to shrink tight to remove any sags and wrinkles.

Corrugated Roofing

DESCRIPTION:
Roofing panels about 26 inches wide and up to 12 feet long. Made of polycarbonate plastic, fiberglass, or metal. Corrugations may be formed with a continuous wave pattern (sometimes called "sine-wave") or have peaks made with three flat surfaces. Available in a range of thicknesses or weights; thicker or heavier generally is stronger. All types available in different colors, while polycarbonate also comes in clear. Metal panels are made of aluminum or with steel that's galvanized or specially coated for corrosion-resistance. Galvanized steel is what's popularly called "tin" roofing, but is not made with tin.

USE:
As awnings over patios, carport roofs, porches, and the like. They let light in but keep out some of the sun's rays and heat. Also commonly used as siding on outbuildings and greenhouses.

USE TIPS:
Plastic and fiberglass panels can be cut with a fine-toothed handsaw or power saws. Metal roofing can be cut with metal shears or with a circular saw fitted with an abrasive metal-cutting blade. Follow the manufacturer's instructions carefully to prevent leaks, cracking due to expansion, and other problems. Best to install using screws with rubber washers.

Plastic Laminate

ALSO KNOWN AS:
Laminate, Formica® (brand name), laminate countertop.

DESCRIPTION:
Hard and brittle ¹⁄₁₆-inch-thick sheet material sold by length and from 24 to 60 inches wide. Standard type has a hard plastic color surface and a base or core that's brown; premium types have the top color going all the way through (called "color core" or "color through"). Plastic laminate has great stain resistance and easy-clean qualities, and, once installed, can take a lot of punishment.

USE:
Still a favorite countertop surface due to its low cost, ease of installation, durability, and other benefits. Countertops are typically built with laminate bonded to a particleboard substrate using contact cement (page 70). Can be cut to rough size with saws or metal shears, then trimmed flush with a router. Also suitable for covering cabinets and walls, but for these and other vertical applications, thinner *roll laminate* (page 81) is typically used.

USE TIPS:
Handle plastic laminate with care before installation. It's very brittle. Also, the edges are extremely sharp when cut or routed and must be filed with a fine file to blunt the razor-sharpness of the plastic.

Roll Laminate

DESCRIPTION:

Plastic laminate in roll form, which is thinner than the better-quality countertop laminate (page 80).

USE:

Best for vertical surfaces that don't require as much durability as countertops.

BUYING TIPS:

Roll laminate is not as good as sheet laminate, but it does work.

Vinyl Patching Kit

DESCRIPTION:

Kit containing patching material, graining "papers," and backing material.

USE:

For repairing holes in vinyl upholstery.

USE TIPS:

Don't expect color-match perfection when using one of these kits.

Fiberglass-Reinforced Plastic (FRP)

ALSO KNOWN AS:

FRP, FRP wall panels/paneling.

DESCRIPTION:

Flexible plastic paneling, about ⅛ inch thick and 4 × 8 feet, with a textured front face. Sold with a variety of plastic moldings for creating a highly washable, water-resistant surface. Installs over drywall with latex mastic or over masonry with oil-based panel adhesive.

USE:

Covering walls behind sinks and toilets and in other wet areas. Commonly used in commercial bathrooms and kitchens but also handy around the house for protecting walls behind mop/utility sinks and laundry rooms or as an economical substitute for ceramic tile around a shower or bathtub.

USE TIPS:

Cuts best with power shears (sheet metal shears), but can be cut with metal snips. Leave about ¼-inch expansion space with all moldings, and seal joints where panel edges meet moldings with silicone caulk, if water-resistance is important.

CHAPTER 11

WINDOW & DOOR SCREEN (AND SUPPLIES)

ABOUT SCREEN MATERIALS

Screening is available in more materials, sizes, strengths, and colors than you probably realize. This may seem like overkill if your cat has torn up the patio screen (again) and you just need a quick fix, but when you understand what's behind the different screen options, they start to make a lot of sense. *Screen weave* denotes the number of strands per inch: standard weave is 18×16, which has 18 strands per inch in one direction and 16 strands in the other direction.

Screening

TYPES:

Fiberglass

Aluminum

Premium metals

Sun control

Pet screen

No-see-um

DESCRIPTION:

FIBERGLASS:

Standard fiberglass screening is the most common screen material on modern windows and doors. Inexpensive and offers good visibility due to minimal glare from sunlight. Won't crease like aluminum and other metal screens. Easiest type to install but also the weakest and most prone to tears and stretching. Commonly available in black, silver gray, and charcoal; black tends to produce the least glare.

ALUMINUM:

The other standard screen material. Offers excellent visibility, but glare can be a problem, especially with shiny gray/silver screen. More rigid than fiberglass and thus a little harder to install but also more durable; less prone to tears and stretching. Be careful not to crease or dent it during installation, as this cannot be fixed. Available in gray, black, and charcoal; black typically is best for visibility.

PREMIUM METALS:

Specialty materials include bronze, stainless steel, copper, and monel (a nickel-copper alloy). All of these except copper are suitable for seaside climates, which cause oxidizing on standard aluminum screen. Premium metals are also desired for a high-end look.

SUN CONTROL:

Also called *solar screen*, *sun screen*, etc. Has thick strands and a special weave that helps block sunlight and solar heat while allowing for decent visibility and keeping out bugs. Often made of PVC-coated fabric strands. Available in a range of colors.

PET SCREEN:

High-strength screen to resist pet claws and paws (also children, who *always* push the screen and never the door frame). Offers poor visibility, so you might want to use this tough screen only on lower portions of doors or windows (unless you have a Great Dane or grown-up children who *still* push on the screen).

NO-SEE-UM:

Also called *small-insect screen*. Similar to standard screen, typically fiberglass, but with a tight 20 × 20 weave to block tiny bugs.

USE TIPS:

Most screen is held in place with screen spline (below). You can reuse old spline, but it gets brittle with age, so it's a good idea to buy new spline along with screen material when replacing old screens. It's also worth it to buy a spline roller tool (page 84) for installing screen and spline.

Screen Spline

DESCRIPTION:

Flexible vinyl cord with fine longitudinal ridges designed to fit into a matching size of channel in screen frames. Comes in diameters of about ⅛ to ⅜ inches and lengths up to 100 feet. Commonly available in gray and black.

Screen spline.

USE:

Securing window and door screen into their frames.

USE TIPS:

Install screen spline with a spline roller (below). If you don't have a spline roller, use a blunt tool to press the spline into the screen frame channels. Don't use a screwdriver or other pointed tool, which will cut through the screen before you know it.

BUYING TIPS:

Spline diameters mentioned above are approximate. In reality, sizes are absurdly precise and include dimensions such as 0.140 and 0.225 inches. But close is good enough; the rubbery spline can be crammed into place as needed. Bring a piece of the old spline to the store for comparison.

Spline Roller

DESCRIPTION:

Simple hand tool with a small metal wheel on each end of a wooden handle. One wheel has a relatively narrow, tapered edge for pressing the screen material into the screen-frame channels. The other wheel has a relatively wide, concave (or channeled) edge for pressing the spline into the channel atop the screening.

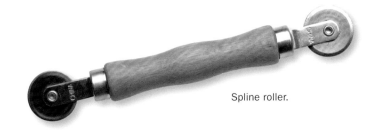

Spline roller.

USE:

Installing window screening and spline.

USE TIPS:

The tapered wheel usually is necessary only for metal screen, which must be pre-pressed into the screen-frame channels prior to installing the spline. Do this gently with a couple of light passes to prevent cutting the screen with the wheel. Standard fiberglass screen can simply be pressed into the channels along with the spline. Use the concave wheel to press and smooth the spline with all types of screen.

BUYING TIPS:

This tool is a true unitasker—it's good for only one job—but it's indispensible for installing screening. Substitute tools tend to cut the screen, and they make it very hard to flatten the spline smooth in the frame channels. Costs only a few bucks, and you'll probably never need to replace.

Screen Frame & Corners

DESCRIPTION:

Bulk lengths of metal screen frame and L-shaped corner pieces—often called *keys*—for joining the frame pieces at the corners. Some keys simply slip into the ends of the frame pieces or clip onto the backsides of the frame corners; others are secured with screws or with peens that you hammer into place with a screwdriver or punch.

Corner keys.

Tilt keys have a small cylindrical post extended from one side for tilt-out screen systems. Frame pieces and keys are sold separately or together as kits.

USE:

Frame pieces and corners are used for building custom-size screens to replace old damaged or missing screens. Frame corners can be used to replace loose or broken corners on existing frames.

USE TIPS:

Frame pieces can be cut to length with a hacksaw. Many corner keys are designed for square-end frame pieces, which means you don't have to make tricky miter cuts for the frame corners.

CHAPTER 12

ROPE & LINE

ABOUT ROPE

Similar to chain and cable, rope is rated for *safe working load*, or a *working load limit* (WLL)—how much weight it should be used to support. It also may carry a rating for *breaking strength*, or *tensile strength*, a weight value based on a laboratory test that stretches the rope until it breaks. The safe working load is only about 20 percent of the breaking strength, so it's important not to confuse the two. Never exceed the safe working load when using rope. Also check the condition of any rope before applying tension to it, because wear, age, dirt, and sunlight can weaken a rope considerably. Knots also reduce a rope's strength—by about 50 percent. The basic options for choosing rope include material, diameter, and weave.

Rope

DESCRIPTION:

MANILA:

Made from hemp. Resists sunlight, doesn't melt or stretch, and ties easily. Like most rope, it is available in diameters ranging from ¼ to ¾ inches and is normally sold by the foot from reels. Because it's a natural material, manila offers limited rot-resistance and is best for use in dry areas. Generally not as strong as synthetic-fiber rope.

1. Sisal rope; 2. Nylon rope; 3. Polyester rope; 4. Polypropylene rope; 5. Manila rope.

SISAL:

Another natural-fiber rope; has less strength than Manila. Best for temporary use or craft projects.

NYLON:

Synthetic-fiber rope offering high strength, rot-resistance and some shock absorption. Suitable for outdoor use. Its big advantage is that it stretches, so if you have a job where the rope may need to take a shock and stretch, by all means use nylon—but beware of jobs where stretching would be a problem.

POLYPROPYLENE:

Synthetic rope that floats and therefore is commonly used as a marker in pools and as a tow rope for boats. Hard to tie. Rot-resistant, but not as UV-resistant as nylon or polyester.

POLYESTER:

Synthetic rope similar in performance to nylon, but not quite as strong; also less elastic, which is an advantage for some applications. UV-resistant and rot-resistant.

USE TIPS:

The ends of all synthetic rope unravels when cut. Melt the fibers with a match flame to prevent unraveling.

BUYING TIPS:

Braided rope generally is much stronger than twisted rope. Braided also offers a better handhold. You can buy rope prepackaged in various lengths, but it's cheaper by the foot, taken off a reel.

Mason's Line

ALSO KNOWN AS:

Builder's line, mason's string, string line.

DESCRIPTION:

Very strong, thin cord, typically made of braided nylon. Usually in a bright color, such as yellow, yellowish-green, orange, or pink, for high visibility. Sold in plain spools or with a winder tool with a handle and spinning spool for easy playing out and winding up of the line. Has some stretch and can be pulled very taut to create straight and level guide lines for various projects.

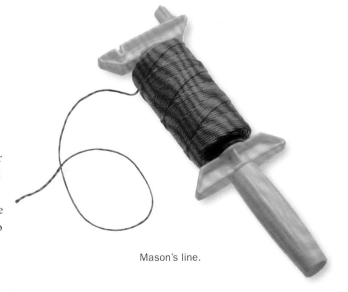

Mason's line.

USE:

Many layout and construction applications. A traditional alignment tool for laying bricks and other masonry. Great for laying out fence posts, patio excavations, garden plots, and outdoor walls. Often used with a *line level*, a small bubble level, to create a level guideline across long distances.

Clothesline

DESCRIPTION:

There are various types. The classic version is braided cotton and has a filler inside to add body and bulk. Other types include plastic (vinyl), braided polyester (or a cotton/poly blend), and vinyl-coated wire or cable. Sold in standard lengths of 50 and 100 feet.

USE:

Hanging clothes to dry, of course, but also a handy all-purpose rope for various household tasks. Do not use clothesline for any kind of weight-bearing application; it's not strong and is susceptible to damage and weak spots, particularly cotton line.

BUYING TIPS:

There's a wide variety of hardware for installing and tightening clothesline, including hooks with integrated mounting plates, line tensioners, pulleys, and clothesline separators (to prevent sagging when running two lines in the same plane).

Twine

DESCRIPTION:

Lightweight rope or cord made of plies twisted just once. There are different kinds: *Polypropylene* is strongest and sometimes the least expensive. *Jute* and *sisal* twine have fuzzy surfaces that bind well when tied.

USE:

Good for lightweight and decorative tying jobs. Jute and sisal are popular in gardening applications because they rot quickly.

Miscellaneous Rope Accessories

DESCRIPTION & USE:

PULLEY:

Grooved wheel held in a housing that has a hook, eye, or bracket for connecting to a rope or piece of hardware or for anchoring to a support. Rope is fed through the pulley and travels along the wheel's groove. Commonly used for clotheslines, but heavy-duty versions can also form the core of a rig winch for hauling up building materials and other tasks. A single pulley makes it easier to lift a weight by reversing the direction of the applied force; it's easier to pull down on a rope than to lift up a weight. Using multiple pulleys on the same rope reduces the force required to a degree proportionate to the number of pulleys.

ROPE SNAPS:

Metal clips, usually with a spring-loaded locking device, for quick connections of rope or line. A few different versions include a *bolt snap* (with or without a swiveling eye), a *snap hook* (a heavier-duty hook with a spring-loaded gate), and a *carabiner* (triangular or oval-shaped clip with a spring-loaded gate).

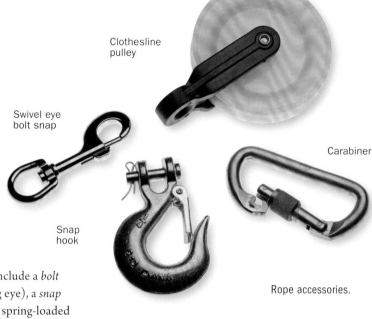

Clothesline pulley

Swivel eye bolt snap

Carabiner

Snap hook

Rope accessories.

USE TIPS:

Carabiners are particularly versatile and easily clip onto many different materials. Although carabiners are standard equipment for rock climbing, cheap utility versions are not very strong and should not be used for load-bearing applications.

Cleat

DESCRIPTION:

Long, narrow metal piece with screw holes on a flat base for anchoring onto a wall or other support structure. Various sizes. A *rope hook*, which has a flat part with screw holes, is used to hold the coiled rope or cord.

USE:

Quick tying of rope or cord, for flagpoles, window blinds, and other applications.

Cleat.

CHAPTER 13

LUBRICANTS

Household Oil

ALSO KNOWN AS:

All-purpose oil, 3-in-1® (brand name).

DESCRIPTION:

Light oil in cans or sprays.

USE:

Lubricating small machinery, doors, and tools around the house. Particularly good for breaking up rust. Cleans and polishes, removes tarnish.

USE TIPS:

Although suitable for most lubrication needs, keep in mind that there are many specialized oils for sewing machines, cycles and mowers, and so on.

Penetrating Oil

ALSO KNOWN AS:

Bolt loosener, easing oil.

DESCRIPTION:

Extremely thin petroleum/graphite mixture in liquid or aerosol spray. Liquid Wrench® is a common brand, as is WD-40®, which comes only as an aerosol spray. Both contain solvents.

USE:

Loosens "frozen" nuts and bolts, "seized" machinery, or corroded galvanized-steel piping when allowed to penetrate for several minutes. WD-40® can be used as a plain solvent as well as a rust preventer on large metal items, such as shovels and lawnmowers. Liquid Wrench® can also be used to remove rust.

Penetrating oil (in use).

After applying penetrating oil, make sure you give it enough time to work. The spray type is good for spots with limited access.

BUYING TIPS:

Liquid Wrench® and WD-40® both make other formulations for various uses, so be sure you have the right item if you ask for it by brand.

Dry Spray Lubricant

DESCRIPTION:

Polytetrafluoroethylene (PTFE; also known as Teflon™) or silicone, available in aerosol cans. Both types go on wet but then dry and cling well to a variety of surfaces. PTFE lubricant doesn't collect dust, making it a good choice for dusty and dirty environments, but is not reliable for outdoor use. Silicone repels water and can be used to dry electrical contacts. A very slick lubricant, best for parts that slide together. Unlike PTFE lube, silicone collects dust.

USE:

Often used to slicken surfaces of drawers, doors, and windows for smoother operation. Works on paint, plastic, wood, glass, leather, and many other surfaces not suitable for liquids. Good lubricant for lock mechanisms.

Synthetic Grease

DESCRIPTION:

High-performance, all-purpose grease. Heat- and water-resistant and long lasting. Similar to conventional petroleum-based grease, but is less prone to breaking down over time. Some formulas are nontoxic and even rated as food-safe.

USE:

Bearings, gears, axles, chains (motor-driven chains, not bike chains), and other moving parts requiring a hard-working lubricant that can handle stress.

Marine Grease

DESCRIPTION:

Thick, waterproof grease for use in wet environments. Effective rust inhibitor; helps prevent against corrosion and seizing parts.

USE:

Metal parts on boats and in marine environments. Trailer axles and bearings. Parts that experience constant outdoor exposure or wetness. Can be submerged in water.

Waterproof Grease

DESCRIPTION:

Highly water-resistant grease for faucet parts. Sold in small tubs and jars.

USE:

Lubricating rubber washers, O-rings, stems, and other parts in faucets. Won't contaminate water supplies.

BUYING TIPS:

There are many varieties of "waterproof" grease, many of which are thick bearing greases designed for cars, motorcycles, and bicycles. These are not suitable for faucets. Be sure the product you use is intended for plumbing fixtures, and is safe for water supplies.

Waterproof grease in plumbing application.

Graphite

DESCRIPTION:

Comes as a powder and is applied with puffer tube.

USE:

Usually used on locks but also good for squeaking floors and stairways.

USE TIPS:

Take care when applying graphite. It can create a mess.

Lock Fluid

DESCRIPTION:

Graphite in fluid or spray form.

USE:

Freeing up lock mechanisms.

Dripless Oil

ALSO KNOWN AS:

White lubricant.

DESCRIPTION:

White, high-viscosity oil—virtually a grease—that will not dry up and become ineffective (as silicone, below, does).

USE:

For hinges and typewriters.

Stick Lubricant

ALSO KNOWN AS:

Stainless stick, stainless lubricant.

DESCRIPTION:

Comes as a grease stick and is applied like a crayon. May be made with mineral oil, wax, or silicone.

USE:

Can be used on metal, plastic, glass, wood. Often advertised as lube for car door hinges. Good for keeping drawers moving freely as well as enhancing the use of drills, saw blades, and other cutting tools.

USE TIPS:

"Stainless" is a misnomer, as oil, wax, and silicone all can stain many materials. A better description is "no-mess." Okay to use on wood, but be aware that the lubricant may inhibit bonding of paint, stain, and other finishes, particularly if the lube contains silicone.

LUBRICANTS

CHAPTER 14

TAPE

Duct Tape

DESCRIPTION:
Reinforced cloth tape with a vinyl backing, commonly 2 inches wide but available in other widths. Also available in a range of strengths—of both the adhesive and the backing—and grades, although the grading is neither official nor consistent. The best indicator of quality is price. In recent years, a few heavy-duty duct tapes have entered the market and offer appreciably stronger adhesive and backing than standard versions.

USE:
Handy for taping almost anything around the house except—notably—ductwork. That's right: standard cloth-and-plastic duct tape is not suitable for taping metal air duct. It'll stick to ducts initially but quickly dries out and looses its grip, failing entirely to create an air seal. The proper tape for ducts is foil tape (below).

BUYING TIPS:
Inexpensive duct tape is not a good buy—the adhesive will be gummy and the tape may slip. Probably one of humankind's most useful inventions. Keep at least two rolls on hand: a good-quality standard duct tape and perhaps a roll of heavy-duty tape for tougher jobs.

Foil Tape

ALSO KNOWN AS:
Metal repair tape, HVAC tape.

DESCRIPTION:
The *real* duct tape, designed to stick to metal duct material and to withstand a wide range of temperature without failure. Has a very strong adhesive and a metal foil backing. Similar widths to standard cloth-and-plastic duct tape. The adhesive side is covered with a non-stick paper strip that you remove as you apply the tape.

USE:
Sealing joints and covering gaps and holes in rigid metal duct, creating an air seal to prevent loss of heated and cooled air in the duct system.

BUYING TIPS:
Make sure your tape is designed for sealing rigid metal duct, if that's your application. Some foil tapes are not up to the job, and there are plastic duct tapes that are rated for flexible ductwork but not necessarily rigid metal duct.

Electrical Tape

DESCRIPTION:

Black tape usually no more than 1 inch wide. Two kinds: one is a fabric that is sticky on both sides, known as friction tape, and adheres only to itself; the other is plastic with adhesive on one side only. The plastic tape stretches quite a bit and thus creates a tightening tension when wrapping wires.

USE:

For wrapping electrical wires, typically for repair or to reinforce electrical connections.

USE TIPS:

Never join wires with electrical tape alone. It's not designed to make electrical connections; it's simply a non-conductive material that covers bare wire or electrical contacts. In most household wiring, wires should be joined together with plastic wire connectors. or wire nuts (page 225). It's ok to apply tape over installed wire nuts, but usually this is not necessary.

BUYING TIPS:

Some tapes look and feel just like electrical tape, although these often come in bright colors, in addition to black. Any tape used on electrical equipment should be called "electrical tape."

Masking Tape

DESCRIPTION:

Paper-backed adhesive tape that comes in various widths up to about 3 inches. The standard size you probably have in your kitchen drawer is ¾ inch wide. This is an all-purpose tape with a relatively strong adhesive. Wider tapes may have weaker adhesive and are designed for masking off windows and other items before painting, although painter's tape (page 96) is better for this job.

USE:

Packaging and general light use. One particularly handy feature of masking tape is that you can write on it with pencil or any kind of pen. It also sticks surprisingly well to most fabrics and works in a pinch to hem pants and patch tears (apply it on the inside of the garment, and burnish the tape well for a good bond).

USE TIPS:

Remove masking tape shortly after use. If left on a surface it tends to leave a gummy residue that can be removed only with a strong solvent such as lacquer thinner. Don't bother with very old masking tape. It doesn't release from the roll well and doesn't stick properly where you want it to.

Painter's Tape

DESCRIPTION:
Paper-backed tape similar to masking tape but with a special adhesive that releases easily when you pull off the tape. This also makes the tape less likely to damage surfaces it's stuck to. Tears easily and has crisp, straight edges, more features that suit its sole purpose.

USE:
Masking off areas prior to painting or other finishing. If you have any masking to do, painter's tape is always worth buying.

USE TIPS:
Like masking tape, painter's tape becomes reluctant to let go if left on a surface for long periods. Also, any paint that overlaps onto the tape can peel off more than you want if the paint is allowed to cure for a long time. Best to remove it as soon as the paint dries.

Painter's tape (in use).

Anti-Slip Tape

ALSO KNOWN AS:
Slip-resistant tape, tread tape, grip tape.

DESCRIPTION:
Heavy tape with gritty surface, available in light and medium duty and in various widths.

USE:
Provides traction for bare feet around pools, on stairways, and in bathrooms.

Carpet Tape

ALSO KNOWN AS:
Double-sided carpet tape.

DESCRIPTION:
Reinforced cloth with adhesive on both sides (one side protected with a removable paper strip).

USE:
Securing carpeting and other flooring.

Flashing Tape

DESCRIPTION:
A thick, rubbery tape, about 6 inches wide and in long rolls with removable film covering the adhesive side. Butyl rubber backing covered with a plastic backing film. Very strong adhesive. When applied, the tape can be stretched to wrap around right angles of window and door frames and even make 90° turns.

USE:
Like metal roof flashing (page 78), this heavy-duty builder's tape keeps water out by bridging over gaps and seams between building components. It's become the new standard for window and door installation, used to cover the sill of window openings or the threshold of door openings before the window or door goes in. After the unit is installed, flashing tape is applied over the flanges of the unit's frame.

Flashing tape.

PART III
PAINTS, STAINS
& OTHER FINISHES

ABOUT PAINT

There is no question that painting jobs are made easier and better when you use top-quality paint (and painting supplies, such as brushes and rollers). Scrimping here is not a good idea. Getting the cheapest paint will almost always yield an inferior job that takes longer, requires more paint, and needs repainting sooner. You can expect to pay more for better-quality paint, but in the end it will cover better, have richer color, and last longer than lower-quality paint. You don't necessarily need to get the premier option or pay extra for so-called "one-coat" formulas (which are a pipe dream in many cases). If you stick with the top one or two grades offered by major brands, you can't go wrong.

Check paint-can labels to get an indication of quality. Paint is made of three components: a *vehicle* (solvent or water); a *pigment* (color); and a *binder*, usually a resin, to hold it all together. Resin can be natural (old-fashioned linseed oil) or synthetic (alkyd, or acrylic polyvinyl acetate). The more pigment and resin the better; likewise, the more vehicle the cheaper it is and the less covering power it has (and what good is paint that won't cover well?). For common household paints, pigment content of about one-third and a vehicle and binder content of about two-thirds is considered good. Ask for the technical specifications sheet.

Regular decorative paints are generally divided into two types: *interior* and *exterior*. Those types are generally available in either alkyd/oil-based or latex/water-based formulas, as explained below. Where you will be using paint (bathroom, ceiling, shingles, etc.) determines what kind of paint you should buy.

A final note: Any paint job can be torpedoed by bad surface preparation. This cannot be overemphasized. Good wall preparation will make any job that much better—and poor preparation will ruin it. In addition to careful surface prep to remove dirt, grime, loose paint, etc., many surfaces should be primed before they are painted (see Interior & Exterior Primer, page 103).

ABOUT LATEX & ALKYD PAINTS

While the overwhelming majority of interior and exterior house paints are latex (water-based), you can still find plenty of alkyd or oil-based paint formulas, and these may be preferable for a some specific applications.

Alkyds, the modern replacement of old-fashioned linseed oil-based paint, are actually a blend of cooked vegetable oils and resins that dry faster and have less odor than the old petroleum oil paints. You can use either alkyd or latex paint for most painting jobs, but not always. These differences are detailed in the items below and on the paint-can labels.

Adding to the confusion is an inconsistency on the part of manufacturers in names. "Latex" is little more than a nickname for water-based paint, as standard paint formulas do not contain latex. Many water-based paints today are called "acrylic," which refers to the type of binder used in the paint. *Acrylic* (and *acrylic latex*) are water-based paints that have acrylic binders.

The basic difference is that alkyd paints are thinned and cleaned up with paint thinner, or turpentine, while latex paints are thinned and cleaned up with warm water, making them mighty popular with the average user. Latex paints dry much faster than alkyd paints, have less odor and fewer noxious fumes (see Buying Tip, below), and are slightly porous to moisture. However, alkyd paints tend to cover a bit better, and are slightly more durable and less prone to showing brush marks. These qualities make alkyd paints the favorite of many professionals for painting furniture, cabinets, and trimwork—particularly when a high-gloss sheen (which tends to show brush marks) is desired.

BUYING TIP

Should you worry about *low-VOC* versus *no-VOC*? Probably not. Most water-based paint these days is relatively low in Volatile Organic Compounds (VOCs). VOCs are chemical compounds found in paint (and other finishes) that are released into the air as vapor during the drying process. Most VOCs escape as the paint is initially drying, which is why you should always paint in a well-ventilated area. VOCs are toxic and can cause headaches, nausea, eye irritation, and other problems (usually when you don't adequately ventilate). They also contribute to ground-level smog as they escape into the atmosphere. Oil-based paints typically have much higher VOC levels than water-based paints. With all that in mind, a lower level of VOCs is a good thing, but you probably don't need to make no-VOC (or zero-VOC) a requirement unless you're particularly sensitive to chemicals.

CHAPTER 15

INTERIOR PAINTS

Standard Interior Paint

DESCRIPTION:

Most commonly water-based paint but also available in alkyd (oil-based) as well as specialty types, such as linseed oil, soy-based, and old-fashioned milk paint. Labeled for interior use. Interior paints are generally available in a variety of sheens—indicating how shiny the paint is when dried. The standard sheens are (from the dullest to the shiniest): flat (matte), eggshell, satin, semi-gloss (medium gloss), and gloss or high-gloss. Sheen categorization and terminology vary by manufacturer, so that what's "eggshell" in one brand might be "satin" in another.

Some paints are labeled as "enamel." This is a loosely applied term but often is used to suggest hardness and/or glossiness. As with sheens, usage varies among manufacturers. The term *latex enamel* is actually a misnomer, as enamels technically are oil-based varnish with pigments.

USE:

Choose a paint sheen based on the application. The higher the sheen the more shiny, washable, and durable the surface. But more sheen also means you get more glare from light and that flaws in the underlying surface are more visible. Flat paint is best for ceilings, which don't need to be washed and should not produce glare. Eggshell and satin are for living-area walls, offering some washability along with reduced glare and soft colors. Semi-gloss is often used for bathroom and kitchen walls, but eggshell or satin also can be used. Gloss is used for wood trim, cabinets, and doors, where maximum durability and washability are desired.

Paint sheens.

USE TIPS:

Flat paints dry lighter than the color on the label, while glosses tend to dry darker. Textured walls often look best with low-glare paint, so opt for eggshell or satin over semi-gloss. A gallon of paint will generally cover 300 to 400 square feet with one coat.

BUYING TIPS:

The best way to judge a paint color is to buy a sample in the sheen you intend to use and paint it directly onto your wall. This is the only way to see how the color is affected by light and is particularly important on highly textured surfaces, which have a lot of reflection and shadowing. Not all paint retailers offer samples in a range of sheens; find one that does.

Interior & Exterior Primer

TYPES:
Alkali-resistant primer
Alkyd primer
Enamel undercoat
Latex primer
Stain-blocking primer

ALSO KNOWN AS:
Sealer, conditioner, undercoater, base coat, primer-sealer, stain killer (stain-blocking primer).

DESCRIPTION:
Primers are almost always a white paint that sticks well to a variety of surfaces. Alkyd is thinned with solvent, latex with water, and shellac-based stain-blocking primer with denatured alcohol.

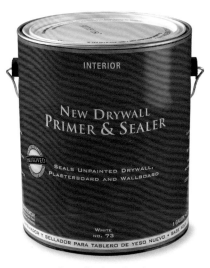

Drywall primer/sealer.

USE:
Providing a good, solid, even base for finish paint, because pigmented finish paints cannot sink in and bond as well as primer. Primer generally is used on previously unpainted (especially porous) surfaces, such as drywall and wood; on surfaces that have been heavily patched; when using high-gloss paint; and when changing from a dark to a light color. Finish paint label will indicate the primer recommended. Stain-blocking primer is used when hiding stains, graffiti, soot, crayon, tape, grease, or knotholes, although some new latex and oil paints have *stain killer* in them. *Block filler* is used on masonry surfaces. *Alkali-resistant primer* is for damp masonry. (Metal primers are covered on page 109.)

USE TIPS:

Any primer helps seal and bond. However, for tough stains and surfaces, use a shellac-based, stain-killing primer (this stuff solves more problems than any other paint). It's great for water stains and seals over crayon, soot, oil-based adhesives (such as that left by old paneling that's been removed), and other materials that easily bleed through ordinary primer and paint. Shellac primers require only one coat and create strong fumes; ventilate the area well.

NOTE:

Nail and screw heads will rust through latex primer unless they are sealed off. Alkyd is best for new drywall that is going to be wallpapered; latex primer should be used if the drywall is going to be painted. Figure coverage of about 250 square feet to the gallon. It is okay to paint over alkyd primer with latex. Primers can be tinted at the paint store to give them a little more hiding power and to make the finish paint "holidays" (missed spots) less evident.

BUYING TIPS:

Primer typically is less expensive than standard paint and tends to stick better to more surfaces. Therefore, applying an extra coat of standard paint instead of a primer coat usually doesn't make sense.

Ceiling Paint

DESCRIPTION:

White, glare-resistant paint in both latex and alkyd formulations, with more and coarser pigment than wall paint.

USE:

For ceilings. Some people use ceiling paint on walls, but it is very dull and not as washable as wall paint; it gives a dead-flat effect. Wall paint is perfectly all right for use on ceilings, but a flat sheen is recommended.

USE TIPS:

Painting ceilings is usually easier if you paint while there is natural light from a window to detect wet, freshly painted areas. If white ceiling paint doesn't cover well, add a teaspoon or two of either lamp black or burnt umber colorant.

BUYING TIPS:

Ceiling paint costs less than wall paint.

Texture Paint

DESCRIPTION:

Thick-bodied paint in various consistencies ranging from relatively thin liquid to material that can be worked almost like grout or mortar. Comes in a few different forms, including: powder that is mixed with water or other base; dry additive, such as sand or perlite, for mixing into the paint of your choice; and in premixed white paints.

USE:

Matching existing textured walls. Hiding badly scarred and cracked ceilings or walls. Also just for decorative purposes, to create various finishes.

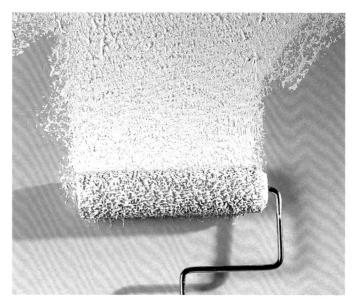

Texture paint applied with a roller.

USE TIPS:

Many different tools, such as crumpled paper, trowels, special paint rollers, and sponges, may be used in working texture paint while wet. If you don't like one effect, you can always rework it. Texture paint is not a cure for badly peeling or flaking paint, as its weight will pull the rest of the old paint off—the cause of the damage must be cured first. Light textures, such as sand or light stippling textures, are easy to apply and tend to yield good results. Thicker textures require expertise; don't expect a heavily textured wall to look like a professional job. Use heavy textures for small patch jobs rather than whole walls or ceilings.

BUYING TIPS:

Because of its thick consistency, coverage per gallon of texture paint is limited. It is therefore expensive, but it does solve minor problems. An alternative to texture paint is to apply spray texture (page 135) to new or patched drywall or plaster, then paint over the texture material.

CHAPTER 16

EXTERIOR PAINTS & STAINS

ABOUT EXTERIOR PAINTS & STAINS

When coating exterior wood (and some masonry) surfaces, you have the choice between paint and stain. Exterior paint is very much like interior paint, but is designed for outdoor exposure. Exterior stain ranges in thickness and opacity: At one end of the range, *solid* stain is nearly identical to paint if perhaps somewhat thinner. At the other end, *semi-transparent* stain can be very thin and lightly pigmented, making it more similar to stain that you might rub onto an indoor furniture project.

Paint is used on all types of siding and outdoor trim materials, while stain typically is used on wood, and specifically on bare wood or previously stained wood. Stain is also the standard choice for decks, fences, and other outdoor wood projects. The particulars of exterior paint and stain are discussed below, but as a general rule of thumb, if you want to preserve some of the natural coloring and texture of real wood surfaces, look at your options for semi-transparent stain; look at solid stain if you want to keep some of the wood texture but not the color.

Like interior paint, exterior paints and stains may be water-based or oil-based. Water-based is preferred by most DIYers for its ease of cleanup and its gentler fumes. It's also somewhat more flexible than oil formulas and can adhere better to more surfaces, including vinyl and aluminum siding. Compatibility with the existing surface is an important consideration. Water-based paint can be applied over water-based or oil-based paint or primer, while oil-based paint should be applied only over oil-based paint or primer. If your house has several layers of old oil-based paint, use oil-based for the new paint job; water-based paint over old oil-based can lead to cracked and peeling paint.

Standard Exterior Paint

DESCRIPTION:
Typically available in the standard range of sheens: flat (matte), eggshell, satin, semi-gloss, and gloss or high-gloss. Flat paint does a good job hiding imperfections and is commonly used on textured siding and trim and on old, weathered siding. Eggshell and satin may be preferred for relatively smooth siding. Semi-gloss and gloss are often used for doors, windows, smooth trim, and other smooth surfaces, such as gutters.

USE:
Painting siding, trim, doors and window, gutters, soffits, and other exterior elements.

USE TIPS:
Application conditions count with exterior paint. The ideal conditions are when the temperature is between 50° and 90°F, there's little or no wind, and you're in the shade. It's worth waiting for these conditions whenever possible. Wind and direct sunlight dry the paint too quickly and make it difficult to apply. Cold temperatures hinder drying and adhesion. Don't paint very early in the morning or late in the evening, because dew can interfere with paint adhesion and drying.

BUYING TIPS:

The best all-around water-based paint for most houses is 100-percent acrylic. It sticks well and lasts longer than most other formulas, including acrylic-vinyl products.

Exterior Stains

TYPES:

Solid (or opaque) stain (also known as *shingle paint*)
Semi-transparent stain
Preservative stain (also known as *waterproofers*)
Specialized stains

DESCRIPTION:

Oil- or water-based, with pigments and additives to resist mildew and moisture. Somewhat like a diluted paint with preservatives. In general, the more solid or opaque a stain is, the more UV protection it provides for the wood. Light, semi-transparent stains offer very little protection from sunlight.

SOLID STAIN:

Like standard paint, imparts an opaque finish.

SEMI-TRANSPARENT STAIN:

Contains less pigment and allows the wood grain to show through.

PRESERVATIVE:

Clear; merely darkens the wood slightly. Intended only for decay-resistance and not used as a decorative finish.

SPECIALIZED STAINS:

Include deck stains, weathering stains, and others.

USE:

Penetrates and preserves exterior wood. Solid and semi-transparent stains are designed for use on all kinds of wood siding. They color the wood to varying degrees and enable it to repel water. Preservatives enable wood to repel water and kill wood-rotting

Waterproofing sealer.

Semi-transparent stain.

Solid-color stain.

organisms, especially for wood in contact with soil or water. Among the specialized stains, deck stains are for application on decks only, while weathering stains give cedar and redwood an aged look upon application.

USE TIPS:
Compared to paint, solid and semi-transparent stain is less forgiving of bad application techniques. The chief problem is *lap mark*—stain dries so quickly that before you can apply a fresh brushfull, the previously applied stain is dry, causing lap marks. The key is to work in small areas quickly, always keeping a wet edge. Also, stir stain frequently to ensure that pigment is properly mixed with the vehicle. Depending on label instructions, it may be applied with brushes, high-nap rollers, or spray. When spraying, always "back-brush"—immediately follow a spray application with a brush or roller to even out the stain and cover any thin or missed areas.

NOTE:
Observe product safety precautions carefully. Many stains and preservatives are highly toxic and create noxious fumes. Rags and other materials containing oil-based products can spontaneously combust if not ventilated properly (seems like an old wives' tale, but this really happens).

BUYING TIPS:
Seek expert advice when choosing a stain. The words "protect" and "protection" are used very liberally on product packaging. Don't underestimate the power of sunlight to discolor and wear wood, and remember that you have to block light to protect wood from UV damage. Clear and lightly pigmented finishes do not block light.

Concrete Stain

ALSO KNOWN AS:
Acid stain, etching stain.

DESCRIPTION:
Acid-based liquid with colorant that penetrates concrete surfaces, adding permanent color through a chemical process. Creates a semi-transparent finish with varied depth of color.

USE:
Decorative finishes for concrete patios, walkways, driveways, and interior concrete floors. The most permanent way to color concrete, especially outdoors. Conventional paint doesn't last long on concrete, and even epoxy paint (page 110) isn't rated for weather exposure. Concrete stain won't wash off or peel like paint can.

USE TIPS:
Follow manufacturer's instructions to the letter. Acid stain is strong stuff and must be mixed and applied properly. Careful surface prep is critical for good results.

CHAPTER 17

SPECIALTY PAINTS

Metal Primers

DESCRIPTION & USE:

ZINC CHROMATE:

White or yellow paint primer thinned with a chemical solvent, such as turpentine. It is used on metal that is inside and not expected to be subject to moisture.

ZINC OXIDE:

Red primer, also thinned with a chemical solvent. Used on metal that will be exposed to moisture.

USE TIPS:

Follow primer labels for how to use the material. Once primed, you can use any finish paint—latex or alkyd—on the metal as long as it's compatible with the primer. Read the label on the paint. Alkyd primer will generally stand up better.

Rust-Inhibiting Paint

DESCRIPTION:

Paint with a rust-inhibiting agent (primer) that is part of the formula of the paint. In other words, the paint is primer and finish paint in one.

USE:

Painting metal.

USE TIPS:

Read the label carefully to ensure that the paint is a primer/finish in one. Some companies make alkyd enamels that are purportedly single-coat metal paints, but they require that a primer be used.

Aluminum Paint

DESCRIPTION:

Aluminum-colored paint consisting of aluminum with a resin base.

USE:

Painting any kind of exterior or interior metal—fences, radiators, sheds, mailboxes, flashing, etc.

USE TIP:

Aluminum paint should be allowed to dry overnight before recoating.

BUYING TIPS:

Cheaper than other metal paints. Great results are easy in spray form.

Epoxy Paint

ALSO KNOWN AS:

Epoxy coating, garage floor paint, epoxy floor paint.

DESCRIPTION:

Paint or coating for interior or garage concrete floors. Comes in two containers, the contents of which are mixed together before use; dries to a hard, glossy finish. May include colorant or color flakes that can be added to mix if desired. Often sold in kits containing applicators.

USE:

Painting porcelain fixtures, such as sinks and tubs, metal, concrete—just about anything.

USE TIPS:

Epoxy is volatile and can be dangerous to use. Read cautionary material on the label and make sure area where you're working is well ventilated. It is not cost-effective to use epoxy where other, less-expensive paints can be used.

BUYING TIPS:

A true epoxy is a two-container material. There are one-container, so-called epoxy enamels but these are not true epoxies and will not perform like the two-container material. "Epoxy paint" typically describes a residential-grade coating that's designed for easy DIY application. Commercial- and marine-grade products are often called "epoxy coatings" and are generally thicker and more durable than epoxy paint and often somewhat more difficult to apply (and more expensive).

Stove Paint

ALSO KNOWN AS:
High-temp paint, high-heat paint.

DESCRIPTION:
Aerosol spray paint designed for high-temperature surfaces, such as wood-burning stoves and vent pipes (chimneys) and barbecue grills. Commonly available in flat-black, but specialty suppliers may offer a range of colors.

USE:
Touch-ups on wood stoves and vent pipes, outdoor grills, smokers, and the like. Some products can be used on stainless steel and other metals.

USE TIPS:
Apply spray paint in three or more very thin coats rather than fewer thicker coats. Follow the manufacturer's instructions for curing the paint. Repeated applications over time can help protect against rust.

Chalkboard Paint

DESCRIPTION:
Flat-black, multi-surface paint that creates a chalkboard-like surface for writing on. Some formulas make the surface magnetic as well.

USE:
Walls, signs, and craft projects.

USE TIPS:
Smooth, hard surfaces work best as chalkboards, for obvious reasons. For a smooth finish, apply the paint in several light coats, using a dense foam roller.

CHAPTER 18

INTERIOR STAINS & CLEAR WOOD FINISHES

ABOUT INTERIOR STAINS

Stains are an alternative to paint when you want the grain of the wood to show. As for which is best to use in which cases, it is often a matter of personal preference. Surface preparation and application are extremely important to a good job, even more so than with paint.

Standard stain penetrates and permanently colors wood fibers, but it does not provide protection from moisture and wear. Some manufacturers combine stain with a protective finish material, such as tung oil or polyurethane, creating an all-in-one formula that not only colors but also seals wood for protection. In most cases, however, a separate protective finish is applied over the stain—even when the stain totally hides the wood.

Getting the results you want from stain can be tricky. The look of stain varies on different woods and even on different areas of the same piece of wood. The only way to see the true color is to try it on the wood itself. That's why it's best to test a stain on a piece of scrap wood or, if you don't have scraps of the same wood, on an inconspicuous area of the furniture piece you will be staining. Also test a second coat, if you're applying one.

Testing stain colors on a hidden area.

Interior Stains

TYPES:
Pigmented stain
Dye stain
Gel stain

ALSO KNOWN AS:

PIGMENTED STAIN:
Pigmented wiping stain, pigmented oil stain, wiping stain.

DYE:
Aniline, spirit stain (if mixed with lacquer or other solvent), water stain, alcohol stain, non-grain raising (NGR) stain (if mixed with certain solvents), penetrating, dye-type.

GEL STAIN:
Heavy-bodied stain.

DESCRIPTION:

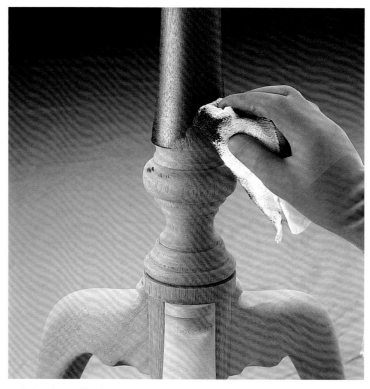

Gel stain application.

PIGMENTED:
Tiny particles of pigment suspended in either oil or latex (latex is water-based but not a water stain). Most common kind—almost like very thin paint. Designed to be brushed on or wiped on with a cloth. Penetrates wood fibers and is typically used only on wood.

DYE:
Aniline dye in powder form, mixed by user with water, oil, or alcohol. When mixed with certain solvents becomes an NGR stain, which dries very fast.

GEL:
Similar to standard pigmented stain but with a thick, gel-like consistency. Unlike standard stain, which soaks into the wood, gel stain coats the surface. This makes it good for woods such as pine and birch,

which have a closed grain that doesn't accept standard stain consistently. Gel stain also is preferred for vertical surfaces because it doesn't run during application. It can be applied to a variety of surfaces, including engineered wood products, such as hardboard, as well as metal and other materials.

USE:

All stains color wood (and other materials, as applicable) and enhance its grain to varying degrees, but provide no protection.

USE TIPS:

Read product label closely for recommended method of application.

PIGMENTED:

Stir constantly, as the pigment never dissolves—it is merely suspended. Wiping-type is easiest to use because you have more control over the rather slow process. Even though the colors are not as pure or transparent as dye stains, the results are quite good and color-fast.

DYE:

Clearest, deepest penetrating colors—but the hardest to obtain and hardest to apply. Tends to raise grain. Surface and NGR types—or any mixed with lacquer, alcohol, or varnish—are hardest to handle and should be left to professionals. Used on the finest hardwoods; not sun-resistant.

GEL:

Generally more foolproof than standard liquid stain. Easier to achieve consistent coloring, particularly on difficult woods. Hides wood grain better than lighter-bodied stain. Sticks to surfaces without running but also collects in corners and crevices. A good option for beginners but only if consistent coloring is more important than highlighting wood grain.

Stain Remover

ALSO KNOWN AS:

Aniline stain remover.

USE:

Removes deeply imbedded stains and water marks.

USE TIPS:

If stains cannot be completely removed, sanding the wood will make it lighter. If it is an alcohol-based or lacquer-based stain, the wood can be lightened slightly by rubbing with denatured alcohol, lacquer thinner, or a mixture of both.

Bleach

ALSO KNOWN AS:

Bleaching solution, wood bleach.

DESCRIPTION:

Liquid product, generally sold in two parts. Similar product but less strong (although poisonous) is *oxalic acid*, which is sold as crystals or powder.

USE:

Applied to bare wood prior to final finishing to produce lighter tones, remove water marks, or to make an uneven surface color even.

USE TIP:

Use caution when working with these caustic products.

ABOUT CLEAR WOOD FINISHES

Technically, paint is just another finish for wood. But when one thinks of wood finishes, one ordinarily thinks of products that allow the wood to show through to varying degrees. There are two basic types of protective wood finish: *surface* and *penetrating*. Surface, or surface-forming, finishes create a continuous, often glossy, layer on top of the wood and offer the most protection from moisture and daily wear. Penetrating finishes soak into the wood surface and harden, forming a lighter protective layer within the wood fibers.

In general, if you want a surface to be washable or, rather, *wipeable* with a damp cloth, use a surface finish. If you want to retain (most of) the feel of the wood and won't leave sweating drink glasses or other wet stuff on the surface, use a penetrating finish.

Clear finishes do one of two things: They protect the wood or, if they have some stain mixed in them, both color and protect it at the same time. However, even the clearest finish will darken wood somewhat. Think of varnish as oil paint without the pigment. Whatever you use, it is always a good idea to test the product on a separate piece of wood or in an out-of-the-way spot to ensure that you will be getting the finish you really want.

ABOUT SURFACE FINISHES

This group of finishes stays right on top of the wood. The coloring of the wood grain shows through, but the finished surface feels more like plastic than wood. Surface finishes typically are applied in multiple thin layers to achieve a buildup.

Polyurethane

ALSO KNOWN AS:

Urethane, poly.

DESCRIPTION:

Available as both a petroleum derivative with a resin base ("oil-based") and in a water-based formula. Very similar to traditional oil-based varnish, of which it is the modern version. Dries quickly, and when thinned can act as its own primer/sealer. Comes in satin or high-gloss, often called *gymnasium finish*.

Polyurethane gloss finishes.

USE:

All-around protective coating for wood furniture, trim, and floors. Resists alcohol, household chemicals, abrasion, and chipping. Most durable finish. Usually applied with a brush or lamb's-wool applicator, but also can be wiped on. Wipe-on formulas are the easiest to apply but create thinner coats than conventional versions, requiring more coats for the same protection.

USE TIPS:

Can outlast traditional varnish two to one. As rugged as it is after curing, polyurethane must be carefully applied and directions for temperature, thinning, and surface preparation followed rigorously. Also, oil-based polyurethane vapors and sanding dust are potentially harmful, so use maximum ventilation and an appropriate respirator. Allow plenty of time for each coat to cure—days in some cases.

BUYING TIPS:

Oil-based versus water-based? Oil-based finishes impart a warm, amber coloring, particularly to light-colored woods, such as oak, birch, and maple. They create stronger fumes and take longer to dry but often require fewer coats. Water-based formulas are clear, less smelly, and they dry faster, but they may need one more coat than oil-based.

Varnish

TYPES:

Alkyd varnish
Spar varnish
Tung oil varnish

ALSO KNOWN AS:

SPAR:

Marine spar, outdoor, phenolic.

TUNG OIL:

Penetrating oil varnish.

NOTE:

The term varnish is sometimes used generically for all clear surface finishes and usually includes polyurethane, which is listed separately here because it is used so widely.

DESCRIPTION:

Various durable formulations with a finish ranging from flat to high-gloss. Regular varnishes take a day or more to dry, but quick-drying, rubbing varnishes take only five hours or so to dry. Some types are also available in water-based formulas.

USE:

Finishing wood trim inside and outside the house.

USE TIPS:

Most varnishes take a long time to dry, so dust can be a problem. Varnish generally needs renewing from time to time. Spar varnish resists sunlight, water (and salt water), and alcohol more than others, but is not recommended for indoor use. Alkyd is less durable.

BUYING TIPS:

The alkyd formulation is least expensive; tung oil the most expensive.

Shellac

DESCRIPTION:

A mixture of a liquid traditionally made from an Indian insect—the lac bug—and alcohol. Currently, artificial substitutes are used as well. Comes as a cream-colored liquid known as *white* shellac as well as an amber-colored one known as *orange*. It is available in a number of different "cuts," referring to the number of pounds of lac flakes, the basic shellac component, per gallon of denatured alcohol. For example, a three-pound "cut" means three pounds of flakes mixed with one gallon of alcohol. Also available in flake form for mixing on location.

USE:

Furniture finish that dries very quickly. Also used as a paint primer/sealer over hard-to-hide colors, patterns, or knotholes.

USE TIPS:

Shellac is not waterproof and responds badly to alcohol; it is also brittle. But as easy as it is to damage, it is easy to repair. It may be waxed for protection too.

BUYING TIPS:

Shellac has a short shelf life. If a can is not dated, test it for clarity and drying time.

Lacquer

DESCRIPTION:

High-gloss finish that dries almost instantly. Thins with lacquer thinner.

USE:

Favored by professional furniture finishers because it dries so quickly. Somewhat similar to varnish. Goes on in thin coats.

USE TIPS:

Apply with spray. It dries too quickly to be applied by brush unless specifically formulated. Somewhat delicate to use for amateurs, except as a touch-up using aerosol spray cans.

ABOUT PENETRATING OIL FINISHES

These finishes are absorbed into the fibers of the wood and actually become part of the wood. They are known for giving the more natural appearance of being "hand-rubbed" and are thus quite different from the surface finishes described above. However, the principle is similar—protecting wood.

Penetrating Oil Finishes

TYPES:

Linseed oil
Tung oil

ALSO KNOWN AS:

BLENDS:

Danish oil, antique oil, Danish penetrating oil, drying oil finish.

TUNG:

China wood oil, China nut oil.

DESCRIPTION:

Oil that penetrates into wood fibers and hardens (polymerizes). Typically leaves a satin finish with a hand-rubbed look. Many different types of blends are available, but most are formulations that include either tung oil and/or linseed oil and solvents and dryers. They often have stains

Penetrating oil application.

incorporated as well. Some of the most popular brands are mostly linseed oil, which costs much less than tung oil. Some purists still use pure linseed or tung oil, but the blends solve a multitude of problems found in the pure oils.

Tung oil is made from the nut of the tung tree, originally found only in China, and is a major ingredient in enamels and varnishes. Many finishes with varying amounts of tung oil in them use "tung oil" in their name, but some might only have a little in them. Check the label.

USE:
Protects wood trim and furniture inside the home. Easy to apply—brushes or wipes on with rag or hand. Very durable—needs little maintenance. Successive layers make for a greater sheen.

USE TIPS:
Some types are safe for surfaces that come into contact with food. Tung oil is highly resistant to water and mildew, and it dries fast. However, it is harder to get good results with pure tung oil than with the many modern penetrating oils that mix tung with various additives to give a much more predictable product. Similarly, linseed oil, squeezed from flax seeds, is the prime ingredient in some of the more popular blends but can also be found pure. It should be "boiled" rather than "raw." Raw linseed oil takes months to dry or may not completely dry at all.

Linseed oil tends to darken with age and need renewal. It is difficult to apply by itself. Like tung oil, it is a common ingredient in other products. Pure linseed oil is not recommended for the average do-it-yourselfer.

BUYING TIPS:
Some brands are available in a combination with stain and sealer for one-step usage. Others are formulated for filling small gaps.

Sealer

ALSO KNOWN AS:
Sanding sealer.

DESCRIPTION:
Clear oil that penetrates deep into wood fibers and seals the surface.

USE:
Protects against grain raising, moisture, and general weathering; as a conditioner and as a primer for varnish, penetrating stain, polyurethane, or high-gloss paints, preventing blotches. Can also be used as a rust inhibitor on metal.

Wood Filler

DESCRIPTION:
Finely ground silex (rock) paste.

USE:
Fills pores of open-grain wood and acts as a primer for varnish, polyurethane, and some lacquer. Can be tinted to match wood.

BUYING TIPS:
Available in oil- and water-based formulas. Oil-based is thicker and easier to apply because of its much longer working time. Water-based is more compatible with a variety of wood finishes.

CHAPTER 19

THINNERS, CLEANERS, REMOVERS & PREPARERS

ABOUT THINNERS

Warning: Thinners are known generally as solvents, or reducers. Most are petroleum distillates and therefore volatile and flammable. Handle with care.

Paint Thinner

ALSO KNOWN AS:

Mineral spirits.

DESCRIPTION:

Petroleum distillate product. Lowest of a number of grades of chemicals distilled from coal, such as benzene, acetone, or naphtha. Extremely volatile and flammable. Generally has only a mild odor.

USE:

Thinning and cleaning up oil-based paints; cleaning up various adhesives and other materials.

USE TIPS:

Avoid splashing in eyes or prolonged contact with skin by wearing goggles and gloves. Avoid diluting final coats of paint; use primarily on prime coats.

BUYING TIPS:

Least expensive of this family of products. Used thinner can be recycled, as paint sinks to the bottom of the container. Don't buy premium-priced "odorless" thinners. It's the paint that smells, and you can't do much about that.

Turpentine

ALSO KNOWN AS:

Pure gum spirits, turps.

DESCRIPTION:

Distilled from pine sap. Slightly lower-quality turpentine, called *steamed distilled* turpentine, is distilled from steamed pine tree bark. Has pronounced odor.

USE:

Thins fine paints; particularly good for thinning exterior oil-based paints, making them easier to apply; general cleanup of all paints. Excellent for cleaning smooth surfaces.

USE TIPS:

Better, quicker, stronger solvent than paint thinner, but has odor.

BUYING TIPS:

Much more expensive than paint thinner, which does most of the jobs that turpentine does.

Lacquer Thinner

DESCRIPTION:

Extremely volatile petroleum-based solvent.

USE:

Cleaning, removing, and thinning lacquer or other oil-based paint products. Cleaning any durable surface, especially removal of tape or adhesive residue.

USE TIP:

Extremely flammable; use with maximum ventilation.

Denatured Alcohol

DESCRIPTION:

Volatile solvent. Ethyl alcohol containing additives that add odor and toxicity (so that people don't drink it, believe it or not).

USE:

Thinning and removing paints and varnishes, removing grease and other smudges, fuel for chafing dishes. Main solvent for shellac.

USE TIPS:

Toxic, but generally safer to use than wood or methanol alcohols, which are strong poisons.

Paint & Varnish Remover

TYPES:
Water wash off remover
Solvent wash off remover
No-wash remover
Latex paint remover

ALSO KNOWN AS:
Stripper, chemical stripper, paint remover.

DESCRIPTION:
All are dangerous, strong chemicals with varying degrees of volatility.

Solvent-based chemical stripper (in use).

WATER WASH OFF:
Liquid or paste containing detergents that allow it to be washed off with water. Very volatile, but nonflammable—unlike other removers.

SOLVENT WASH OFF:
Liquid or paste that is washed away with solvent—either a petroleum distillate or denatured alcohol.

NO-WASH:
Remover that can be merely wiped off surface with an absorbent cloth.

LATEX PAINT REMOVER:
Solvent or water-based chemical that acts only on latex, not oil-based, paints.

USE:
Removes paint, varnishes, and other finishes from wood. Typically, the remover is applied, allowed to remain a specified time, and then it—and the old finish—is scraped off. Latex paint removers also remove crayon, tape residue, gum, and grease.

USE TIPS:
Removers work, but most are messy and include dangerous, very strong chemicals. Read labels carefully for cautions. Use proper safety equipment: goggles and heavy rubber gloves, long sleeves and long pants, and adequate ventilation; and keep a water source ready in case you get some caustic chemical on your skin. Do not use in direct sunlight. Note that other, safer chemicals may be able to remove finishes. For example, denatured alcohol will remove shellac, as well as some varnishes. Lacquer thinner takes off lacquer. Heat removes paint (but not varnish) very well, through the use of heat guns or plates, and it is not toxic—though

the old paint may be. Use a liquid remover only on horizontal surfaces, or it will run off. A paste remover can be used on vertical and horizontal surfaces. Water-based strippers raise the wood grain. Plastic abrasive pads are excellent substitutes for steel wool when removing gooey paint residue.

BUYING TIPS:

There are many different removers available, ranging from high to low toxicity and even "nontoxic," which does *not* mean it's okay if ingested or gets in your eyes. Generally, the strongest chemical formulas work the fastest but are the most toxic. Strippers containing methylene chloride (dichloromethane) typically are the most toxic and noxious, followed by those made with N-Methylpyrrolidone (NMP). "Safe" stripper formulas may be sufficiently low-toxicity to use indoors, and include citrus-based and soy-based formulas.

Wood Scratch & Hole Fillers

TYPES:

Color stick
Lacquer stick
Liquid colorant
Shellac stick
Wood putty
Wood patch

ALSO KNOWN AS:

WOOD PUTTY:

Wood dough, Plastic Wood® (brand name; premixed type), wood patcher, wood patching compound, wood filler.

DESCRIPTION:

COLOR STICK:

Relatively soft, crayon-like stick in various wood colors.

LACQUER & SHELLAC STICKS:

Lacquer and shellac in hard stick form. They come in a variety of wood colors and are melted for use.

LIQUID COLORANT:

Aniline dyes in small bottles in various colors.

WOOD PUTTY:

Permanently soft putty often made of fibers and adhesives, available in a range of wood colors, sold in small containers. Wood Putty™ is also a brand name.

WOOD PATCH:

Paste that hardens and may or may not be paintable and stainable, water (latex) or solvent-based, quick-setting or not, or is a two-part epoxy or polyester compound. Water Putty® is a brand name for a gypsum-based (plaster) powder that is mixed with water and quickly becomes extremely hard.

USE:

Shellac, lacquer stick, and *water putty* are for holes, though they can also be used on deep scratches. *Color sticks* and *dyes* are for scratches; the former is rubbed over the scratch while the latter is applied with a tiny brush.

BUYING TIPS:

Powdered water putty is amazingly useful. Unused portions can be stored indefinitely (the premixed kind tends to dry out), and it can be used for large holes and even as a floor leveler. No worker should be without a large can.

Sandpaper

ALSO KNOWN AS:

Abrasive paper, coated abrasive, garnet paper, production paper.

DESCRIPTION:

Sandpaper is made in various degrees of coarseness, with different abrasive materials adhered to various backings. Some (the very finest grades) can be used dry or wet—that is, moistened with water or oil. This keeps the dust down and acts as a lubricant to prevent scratches on very smooth or polished surfaces. Sandpaper comes described both by number—either of two kinds—and verbally. With either system, the higher the number, the finer the grit of the paper. The range commonly available includes:

Very fine (8/0 to 6/0, or 280- to 220-grit)
Fine (5/0 to 4/0, or 180- to 150-grit)
Medium (3/0 to 1/0, or 120- to 80-grit)
Coarse (1/2 to 1 1/2, or 60- to 40-grit)

Extreme ranges include grits of 12 on the coarse end and upwards of 2,500 on the fine end of the scale. Grit numbers refer to the size of the abrasive grains themselves; the numbers are higher for finer grades because there are more pieces of grit per square inch.

This classification is only relative and varies somewhat from manufacturer to manufacturer and material to material. Remember that the grit, or mesh, is your most accurate guide from brand to brand.

Sandpaper also comes with *closed* and *open* coat, meaning the grit is farther apart or closer together. If closed coat, the grit covers 100 percent of the surface; with open coat, the grit may cover only 60 to 70 percent. Open coat tends to clog up less with sawdust, which is a big advantage on belt sanders, and it lasts longer, but closed coat will cut faster.

Three common kinds of paper are *flint* (least durable and least expensive), *emery* (called *emery cloth* or *emery paper*), and *aluminum oxide* (most common). Flint is cream or tan; emery, black; and aluminum oxide, a reddish color. The weight—the thickness or stiffness of the backing material—is designated by letters. Paper backing is rated A to E, thin to thick; C or D is usually best. Cloth backing is rated J or X; J is thinner and more flexible, while X is thicker and used for heavy-duty and power sanding.

Sandpaper is available in many forms, including the familiar 9 × 11-inch sheets, peel-and-stick or Velcro-backed pieces for easy adhering to power sanders, and sanding sponges that work as handy sanding blocks and have beveled edges for reaching fine edges and tight corners.

USE TIPS:

For even hand-sanding, wrap sandpaper sheets around a wood block (or an old sanding sponge) for flat surfaces and straight edges, or around a wood dowel for sanding curves. Many common materials, some types of paint, plaster, and treated wood, yield a toxic sanding dust. Use wet sandpaper and/or a respirator, as applicable.

Steel Wool

DESCRIPTION:

Steel thread of various thicknesses loosely woven into hand-sized pads; also sold in bulk packages. *Bronze wool*, also available, is simply steel wool made of bronze. Now, synthetic steel wool (also known as *abrasive nylon pads* or *sanding pads*) is widely available. Pads are made from synthetic fibers and abrasive particles in various thicknesses; they resemble dishwashing scouring pads.

USE:

Steel wool is used for a variety of purposes, including a final wiping of wood and other surfaces prior to finishing, taking the gloss off a surface prior to painting or finishing, removing hardened substances such as dried paint, and applying final finishing materials, such as wax.

Steel wool comes in six or seven grades ranging from 0000 (super-fine), through 000 (extra-fine), 00 (very fine), 0 (medium fine), No. 1 (medium), No. 2 (medium coarse), and No. 3 (coarse).

USE TIPS:

Bronze, stainless steel, and synthetic pads are better for use with water-based finishes, as loose strands will not rust. Fine steel wool is great for putting a shine back on old metal parts and can even be used to clean window glass (with 0000 wool only).

BUYING TIPS:

For removal jobs, synthetic steel wool is the way to go. It won't shed, splinter, or rust. It can be rinsed and reused a few times, and it is generally longer lasting, safer, and cleaner to use.

PART IV
WALL, CEILING &
FLOOR REPAIR MATERIALS

CHAPTER 20

DRYWALL & PLASTER PATCHING MATERIALS

ABOUT DRYWALL & PLASTER REPAIR

Both drywall and plaster are made with gypsum—the chalky, white dust that drizzles all over the floor whenever you drill into your wall or ceiling. Because of this, drywall and plaster can be repaired with the same materials, by and large. If you're just filling holes left over from hanging pictures or curtain hardware and the like, use some spackling compound. This is also the best stuff to have on hand when prepping walls and ceilings for a new paint job. For pretty much every other type of wall or ceiling repair, you can use drywall joint compound or patching plaster.

Large holes that go through drywall or plaster usually call for a patch of new drywall or a drywall patch kit. Seams around drywall patches should be covered with drywall joint tape and coated with three layers of drywall compound. You can also use compound to create a texture to blend repairs into the surrounding area.

Joint Compound

ALSO KNOWN AS:
Drywall compound, drywall mud.

DESCRIPTION:
Available as premixed paste and in powder form that is mixed with water. Comes in three main types: *setting* (or taping), *topping*, and *all-purpose*. Setting-type dries fast and hard and is used most commonly for the first coat over drywall joint tape (page 131), when finishing new drywall. Topping is a lighter, softer formula used for the finish coats over the taping coat. These two types are most commonly used by professionals when finishing new drywall installations. However, setting compound is also suitable for plaster and drywall repairs in relatively small areas. All-purpose compound is softer (and a bit easier to work) than setting-type and is harder than topping-type, so it's used for both taping and finish coats, as well as general repairs.

USE:
Sealing drywall joints with joint tape as well as extremely shallow patching, such as in areas where paint has peeled. Intended for use over wide areas in thin, successive coats. A number of applications will likely be required because joint compound shrinks as it dries. Must be primed (with primer or flat latex paint) prior to painting.

USE TIPS:
Joint compound works best when applied in multiple thin layers to prevent excessive shrinking and cracking of the compound. Apply with a 4-inch putty knife (for very small areas) or a 6-inch or wider drywall knife, smoothing each layer with the knife and feathering it out beyond the previous coat. Smooth each coat further

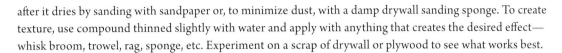

after it dries by sanding with sandpaper or, to minimize dust, with a damp drywall sanding sponge. To create texture, use compound thinned slightly with water and apply with anything that creates the desired effect—whisk broom, trowel, rag, sponge, etc. Experiment on a scrap of drywall or plywood to see what works best.

BUYING TIPS:

Premixed all-purpose joint compound is typically recommended for DIYers because it's already mixed to the proper consistency and it has a long working time before it sets up. However, it usually has to dry overnight and, while it stores well, the compound in the container eventually dries out too. If you need only a little compound here and there and/or you're pressed for time, consider a dry mix of setting-type compound. This can set in as little as 15 minutes (the number on the bag indicates the working time) and often can be recoated or painted in just a few hours. The dry mix lasts forever in storage as long as it doesn't get wet. Mix batches with small amounts of water to the consistency of warm peanut butter. A potato masher speeds mixing and prevents lumps (rinse off all the mud before putting the masher in the dishwasher).

Joint Tape

TYPES:

Paper tape
Fiberglass mesh tape

ALSO KNOWN AS:

Wallboard tape, drywall tape.

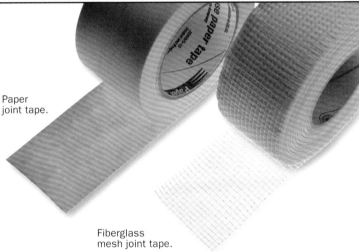

Paper joint tape.

Fiberglass mesh joint tape.

DESCRIPTION:

Two-inch-wide paper or fiberglass mesh strip sold in rolls of various lengths. Paper tape is non-adhesive and has a crease down the middle to facilitate folding it in half lengthwise to apply to inside corners of walls or ceilings. It must be applied over a continuous layer of joint compound (page 130) to adhere it to the wall or ceiling surface. Fiberglass mesh is self-adhesive and is applied the wall or ceiling surface before being covered with joint compound. *Cementboard* or *alkali-resistant* mesh tape is a special type of joint tape for use with cementboard (tile backer) and the cement-based mortar used to cover cementboard joints.

USE:

Always used in conjunction with joint compound, joint tape is essential to creating lasting finishes over joints (seams) in drywall panels and repairs. It can also span over small holes (up to about 2 inches in diameter, such as the dimple created by a doorknob) to eliminate the need to install a drywall patch.

USE TIPS:

For beginners, fiberglass mesh is much easier to use than paper tape, because you can stick it to the wall and add a thin layer of joint compound whenever you're ready. Paper tape must be embedded in an even layer of wet compound, then smoothed and flattened carefully with a drywall knife, pushing out just the right amount of mud from behind the tape. Because mesh-tape joints generally are not as strong as paper-tape joints, manufacturers recommend using setting-type joint compound for at least the first layer over mesh tape. However, strength is more important for new drywall panel installation and for joints over doors and windows (which tend to move and crack) than it is for patches, holes, and other basic repairs.

Patching Plaster

ALSO KNOWN AS:

Wall patch, plaster patch, plaster of Paris, painter's plaster.

DESCRIPTION:

Plaster-based paste commonly sold as a dry powder that you mix with water. Contains additives to make it more workable, and to give it a longer set time than traditional wall plaster or plaster of Paris. Applied to wall or ceiling with a trowel, typically in one application. Sets in approximately 90 minutes. *Plaster of Paris* is the generic name for a very common product made of ground-up and treated gypsum rock (originally mined near Paris).

USE:

PATCHING PLASTER:

Filling large cracks and breaks in plaster surfaces, but not holes. Similar to setting-type joint compound but better for repairing large defects, because it can be applied thicker. Not suitable for molding/casting.

PLASTER OF PARIS:

Reconstructing plaster molding and other details; filling very large patches; anchoring ceramic bathroom fixtures; hobby projects, such as molding and casting (check the product literature; not all plaster of Paris should come in contact with skin).

USE TIPS:

Dampen surfaces before applying, or use a bonding agent (page 133), to ensure adhesion to old plaster and lath (the wood strips that hold the plaster to the wall or ceiling framing). Use patching plaster for repairing large defects, not for fine cracks (use spackling compound instead) or for smoothing over broad areas (use all-purpose joint compound).

Spackling Compound

ALSO KNOWN AS:

Spackle® (brand name), spackling, spackling paste.

DESCRIPTION:

Lightweight, gypsum-based paste. Extremely fast setting and nonshrinking. Sold in tubs, tubes, and even pencil-like dispensers. The verb "to spackle" comes from the German verb *spachteln*, meaning to fill or smooth a surface; Spackle is a brand name that is used—incorrectly—in a generic way for this family of products.

USE:

Filling small and/or shallow holes and depressions in drywall and plaster surfaces. Applied with a putty knife or small drywall knife, or by hand for small nail and tack holes. Ideal for quick, single application prior to painting.

BUYING TIPS:

"Lightweight" spackling compound is almost fluffy and dries so fast it can be painted in about 15 minutes, but it doesn't spread smoothly like standard spackling. Use lightweight for nail and screw holes, smoothing it flat with a putty knife or even your finger.

Bonding Agent

DESCRIPTION:

Resinous emulsion that is brushed or rolled onto wall surface and allowed to dry until it becomes tacky.

USE:

Dramatically increases bonding of new plaster or cementitious material to any structurally sound surface. Virtually welds the patch to the old material. Useful for repairing cracks in and gaps of peeling paint on old plaster.

USE TIPS:

While it is necessary to wait until this becomes tacky, it is okay to wait as much as two weeks after application to apply the plaster to it.

BUYING TIPS:

Yields excellent results. Some types are made specifically for plaster or concrete, while others work with both or are marked for interior or exterior use. Check the label carefully.

Self-Adhesive Wall Patch

ALSO KNOWN AS:

Metal drywall repair patch.

DESCRIPTION:

Four- to eight-inch square piece of fiberglass mesh with adhesive backing, containing a perforated aluminum plate in its center. Peel-and-stick *patching tape* has no metal and is slightly flexible.

USE:

Patching large holes in drywall, plaster, or hollow-core doors with a minimum of patching material. The aluminum eliminates the need to fill the hole with drywall, and the adhesive mesh eliminates the need for pre-mudding. Smaller versions, made only of very stiff mesh, are specifically designed to bridge the gap between drywall and electrical boxes, a gap that is particularly hard to fill without cracking. They are placed over the entire hole and then the inside is cut out to leave the electrical box open while providing surface around it for patching compound. *Patching tape* is for small holes and cracks in plaster.

Drywall Repair Clip

DESCRIPTION:
Small, perforated, flat metal clip with openings on opposite sides.

USE:
Provides instant bracing for repair of large holes in drywall. The "filler" piece of drywall is simply clipped in place and then covered with patching compound. Eliminates the need to cut back the surrounding drywall to the nearest studs or to install wood bracing.

Spray Texture

DESCRIPTION:
Wall/ceiling texture in a can. Aerosol spray containing a paint-like medium and filler material for instant texturing of wall or ceiling surfaces. Simulates the spray equipment used by professionals to create various effects.

USE:
Texturing patches and repairs to blend them with the original surface texture. Different formulas available for recreating various popular textures, including orange-peel, knockdown, and popcorn (acoustical) textures.

USE TIPS:
Works pretty well for areas up to a few square feet. Is not suitable for texturing an entire wall or ceiling of new drywall (call a pro for that). Always test the texture on a clean scrap of drywall or cardboard. Shake can well before application. If you don't like how it looks on the wall, scrape it off with a drywall knife or wide putty knife while it's still wet. Let the surface dry, then try again.

CHAPTER 21

INTERIOR FLOOR REPAIR MATERIALS

Vinyl Seam Adhesive

ALSO KNOWN AS:

Vinyl repair adhesive.

DESCRIPTION:

Special glue for vinyl (resilient) flooring. Sold in a squeeze bottle with a pointed applicator tip. Most types are washable with a wet rag.

USE:

Vinyl flooring repairs, including installing patches to replace damaged areas and resticking loose edges and seams.

USE TIPS:

Clean the repair area thoroughly before applying adhesive. Roll flooring with a seam roller (wallpaper seam roller) to flatten and smooth the vinyl and create a strong bond. Repair damaged flooring by replacing area with a patch of leftover flooring (if you have some; if not, remove a piece from under an appliance or other inconspicuous area). Place the patch material over the floor and double-cut through both layers to create a perfectly sized patch.

Flooring Repair Kit

ALSO KNOWN AS:

Floor and tile repair kit, vinyl repair kit.

DESCRIPTION:

Liquid or paste compound made with vinyl, acrylic, or similar materials. Essentially a hole-filler that dries to a hard finish and can be painted or stained and sometimes textured. Kits may include special applicators, mixing vessels, colorants (for mixing custom colors), or texture paper (a textured film for embossing the repair material to match flooring).

USE:

Repairing small tears, holes, and gouges in vinyl, linoleum, ceramic tile, wood, and laminate flooring. Some formulas can be used on laminate countertops. Kits specifically for laminate and wood flooring often include a clear lacquer for sealing over the repair and blending with prefinished or polyurethane-coated flooring.

Carpet Seam Tape

DESCRIPTION:

Wide, double-sided tape designed to stick to subflooring on the bottom side and carpet backing on the top side. Various types available, including thin plastic versions, heavy-duty types with mesh backing, and traditional hot-melt tape that requires a carpet seaming iron to melt the adhesive. Also types are available specifically for indoor/outdoor carpet.

USE:

Repairing or reattaching loose carpet seams and edges, installing carpet patches.

Pressure-sensitive carpet seam tape.

BUYING TIPS:

The best type for installing carpet repair patches or securing loose seams is pressure-sensitive tape with a heavy-duty mesh backing. It's strong and bonds well to carpet backing without the need for heat.

Tile Repair Adhesive

DESCRIPTION:

Water-based adhesive in a caulking-type tube, applied with a caulk gun. Similar look and consistency to standard white school glue.

USE:

Filling voids under tile (ceramic, porcelain, stone) and bonding tile to substrate to eliminate hollow sound or to re-adhere loose or rocking tile. Adhesive is squirted into holes drilled through the grout joints surrounding the problem tile. Cleans up with water. Holes are filled with matching grout to complete repair.

Tile Adhesive

TYPES:

Mastic
Thinset

DESCRIPTION:

Two types of adhesive for installing ceramic, porcelain, or stone tile. Mastic is a latex (usually water-based but may be solvent-based) formula that comes premixed in plastic tubs. It's typically used for wall tile. Thinset is a cement-based powder that you mix with water, typically used for floor tile and always for tile laid over concrete or cementboard.

USE:

Installing tile for repairs or new installation.

USE TIPS:

Both mastic and thinset are applied with a notched trowel, which spreads the adhesive in V-shaped or square-edged channels. This helps the tiles lie flat—at the right height—and aids adhesion by creating a suction effect. You can spread the adhesive with a putty knife, but if you use too much or too little, the tile will sit too high or low. Scrape out oozed adhesive from grout joints before it dries.

BUYING TIPS:

Small plastic containers of thinset are handy for repairs. They have extra space for adding water and mixing right in the container, which is discarded when you're done.

Grout

DESCRIPTION:

Cement-based mortar sold in dry powder that you mix with water. Forms a gritty paste with consistency of peanut butter. Comes in *sanded* and *unsanded* (non-sanded) versions. Sold in large bags and various tub sizes in a range of colors.

USE:

Filling the joints (spaces) around ceramic, porcelain, and stone tile. Used when installing new tile, replacing broken or loose tile, or replacing just the grout around well-adhered tiles.

USE TIPS:

Mix grout by adding water to the dry powder and stirring until entirely moistened, then let the mixture sit for about ten minutes (called "slaking"). Stir the mixture again just before applying, but do not add more water. Grout sets up in about 15 minutes after slaking, so work quickly. Apply with a grout float or, if you have just a tile or two to fix or very small joints, you can use your finger.

BUYING TIPS:

Sanded grout is most commonly used for floor tile or any grout joints ⅛ inch wide and wider. *Unsanded* grout is for joints under ⅛ inch wide. Bring a chunk of the old grout with you to the store to find the best color match.

CHAPTER 22

CONCRETE FLOOR & WALL REPAIR MATERIALS

ABOUT CONCRETE REPAIRS

Repairing concrete is largely a cosmetic effort, as concrete slabs and walls are massive monolithic structures that can't be fixed with surface treatments. That said, patching holes and filling cracks in concrete can help forestall or prevent further damage by keeping out water that can freeze and expand inside the cavities, and to keep out weeds and soil.

Repair materials include various concrete mixes, cement-based mortars with special additives, thin surfacing mixtures, and caulks and sealants. Often, the appropriate material is determined by the thickness of the repair. For example, standard bagged concrete contains large gravel and is thus suitable for repairs that are over ½ inch in thickness. Caulks are suitable for narrow cracks, while wide cracks call for a cementitious mortar product that locks itself into place.

Despite popular usage, *cement* and *concrete* are not the same thing. Cement is merely the glue, or binder, in concrete, mortar, and grout mixes. Concrete is a blend of cement, gravel and/or sand (known as aggregate), and sometimes additives that add strength, workability, and other properties.

Concrete & Mortar

DESCRIPTION:

Premixed concrete and mortar mixes are sold in 10- to 80-pound bags and are mixed with water. *Standard concrete* contains both gravel and sand and offers the most strength. *Sand mix concrete* has only sand (no gravel) as its aggregate. It can be spread thinly and fill small voids, but it's not as strong as standard concrete. *Mortar* is also a blend of fine sand and cement and comes in various types for specific applications. Various types are available for special purposes. Strength rated according to type M (strongest), S, N, O (weakest).

USE:

STANDARD CONCRETE:

Used for all sorts of construction projects, including slabs, walls, steps, curbs, and deck footings. Fast-setting mix is favored for anchoring fence posts, because it cures more quickly than standard concrete. Can be used to rebuild broken steps and other structures as well as fill large holes.

SAND MIX CONCRETE:

Used for repairing cracks, holes, and other small masonry patching jobs. Sometimes used for concrete overlay—a ½- to 2-inch-thick layer of new concrete over an old concrete slab or walkway. Also useful for casting projects with fine detail, where gravel in standard concrete would be problematic.

MORTAR:

Used for repairing (tuck-pointing) or making mortar joints in brick and concrete block. Various types and strengths have different uses: type M is the strongest, followed by types S, N, and O (the weakest). Type S is typically used for brick walls, and type N for concrete block.

USE TIPS:

Proper mixing is critical to making concrete and mortar workable and ultimately strong. Too little water makes it crumbly and hard to work with; too much water makes it soupy and weakens the finished product. Add small amounts of water to the dry mix until the proper consistency is achieved. Concrete cures (hardens) through a chemical process and should not be allowed to dry too quickly. *Latex masonry adhesive* or emulsion can be added to sand mixes to increase bonding ability and curing quality.

Cement & Concrete Patchers

TYPES:
Anchoring cement
Epoxy cement
Hydraulic cement
Latex cement
Standard cement
Vinyl patching cement

DESCRIPTION & USE:
Cement mixed with a bonding agent and other additives that increase adhesion strength and allow for thin-setting ability. Some are ready-to-use, others need water.

ANCHORING CEMENT:

Also known as *expanding cement*. Slightly expanding, fast-setting cement, ready to use, although some brands need water added. Used for anchoring metal railings and gate posts, fences, and bolts. Slower setting than hydraulic cement.

EPOXY CEMENT:

Comes as a bag of dry cement, hardener, and emulsion that is mixed together before use. May be used to patch any kind of material, including glass and steel, particularly where strength is important, and may be used to set flagstone and other patio paving materials.

HYDRAULIC CEMENT:

Comes as a powder. Similar to anchoring, but faster setting. Expands as it cures to fill cracks tightly. Applied directly to a water leak in masonry and quickly hardens in place. Commonly used to fill and seal cracks in concrete basement walls and retaining walls.

LATEX CEMENT:

Powder mixed with a latex liquid before use. Can be troweled to $\frac{1}{16}$-inch thickness. Excellent adhering power. Used for smoothing rough surfaces and repairing hairline cracks.

STANDARD CEMENT:

Blend of cement and sand that is mixed with water. Used for repairing small holes and cracks; cracks need to be undercut first to create a "key" that the repair can lock into.

VINYL CEMENT:

Powder mixed with water. Can be troweled to $\frac{1}{8}$-inch thickness. Excellent adhering power, more than regular cement and sand mixtures. Used to repair small cracks in concrete, glass, marble, tile, and brick. Vinyl bonding is strong.

USE TIPS:

Surfaces should be well cleaned using a *concrete cleaner*, *etching material*, or *degreaser* before application of patchers.

BUYING TIPS:

Epoxy is the most expensive patcher. Acrylic, resinous, or latex bonding agents or adhesives are also sold separately as additives or primers.

Masonry Sealers

TYPES:

Acrylic resin sealer
Bituminous sealer
Cement latex sealer
Cement mortar
Epoxy resins
Silicone

ALSO KNOWN AS:

Masonry waterproofers, waterproofers, waterproof cement paint.

DESCRIPTION:

Many proprietary formulations. Most common are:

ACRYLIC RESIN:

Rubber and Portland cement mixture applied by brush.

BITUMINOUS:

Thick, black tar-like material that can be applied hot or cold.

CEMENT LATEX:

Cement-based with latex additives.

CEMENT MORTAR:

Composed of one part water and one part cement.

EPOXY:

Synthetic material that sets very quickly.

SILICONE:

Highly viscous material that goes on like paint.

USES:

To seal masonry walls against moisture penetration, dusting, staining, spalling, and the effects of weather. Decorative, as well. Bituminous may be used as a roof coating.

USE TIPS:

Before using a waterproofer, make sure that the problem is moisture intruding through the walls and not condensation due to moisture inside the building. Always try to cure the source of the moisture. Follow surface preparation directions exactly. Note if product requires use of *etching* and *cleaning compound*. Most sealers won't work over old paint. Take precautions to avoid eye and skin irritations as specified on the label.

BUYING TIPS:

Quality sealers penetrate and swell to become an integral part of the masonry, not just a surface coating. Some products contain a mildewcide too. Some have better white tones than others; check regarding colors. Application may include special additives.

Concrete Caulk

ALSO KNOWN AS:

Crack filler, concrete sealant, concrete repair caulk.

DESCRIPTION:

Exterior-grade caulk formulated for concrete and other masonry materials. Various types include acrylic, silicone, and urethane. Some caulks contain sand for texture. Many are thinner than standard caulk and are self-leveling, so they spread out into a smooth plane when applied to horizontal surfaces.

USE:

Filling cracks and expansion joints in concrete floors, driveways, patios, walkways, and walls, as well as other masonry structures.

USE TIPS:

Fill wide and/or deep cracks and joints with backer rod (foam rope sold in various diameters) before caulking the crack. Tuck the rod into the crack so it is about ½ inch below the concrete surface, then caulk directly over the rod, making sure the caulk completely bridges the gap.

BUYING TIPS:

You get what you pay for. High-performance caulk (many of these are urethane) lasts many times longer and stays more flexible than low-quality products.

Foam backer rod.

PART V
PLUMBING SUPPLIES

A NOTE ABOUT PLUMBING CODES

When planning a plumbing project and choosing products to buy, take into account local building and plumbing codes. These are sets of rules and regulations enforced by the local building authority—usually part of your city's building department—and they govern what products may be used and how the installations must be done. Similar codes exist for electrical and general construction work.

If you're just replacing some old parts with identical or similar new parts, you probably don't need to check the code. But if your project involves significant replacement or modification of what's there, or if you're installing new plumbing (particularly any new supply, drain, or vent lines), it's important to know the code requirements that apply. Also be aware that code rules change over time; what might have been "code" when your house was built may not be code today. And the general rule is that any modifications or updates you make to existing work must be done to code.

Plumbing codes have a simple purpose: to ensure that the installed plumbing is done safely and does not jeopardize the health of a building's occupants. However, despite this seemingly straightforward goal, plumbing codes vary greatly from community to community, sometimes in a contradictory manner. But they must be followed. If they are not, a plumbing inspector (on a project that requires a permit) can order the removal of any installation that violates the code, even though the installation may be perfectly safe. If your project requires a permit but you don't get one (and thus code violations aren't caught by a city inspector) you can still get flagged for faulty work—by the house inspector when you try to sell your house.

The local building department can tell you what types of plumbing projects need permits and where to find the relevant code information. Local plumbers usually know the same.

CHAPTER 23

PIPE & ACCESSORIES

ABOUT PIPE & FITTINGS

There are two kinds of pipe in a house: *water supply* and *waste*. Water supply pipe (sometimes called distribution pipe) supplies cold water to the house from the city main or well and distributes hot and cold water inside the house. Waste pipe transports waste, "used," or soiled, water to a sewer, septic tank, or other disposal facility. Water piping inside the home typically is ¼ to ¾ inches in diameter; waste is bigger, typically ranging from 1¼ to 4 inches.

Water supply pipe is also known as *supply pipe* or simply *water pipe*. Waste pipe is also known as *drainage pipe, soil pipe, sewer pipe, drain pipe, drain-waste-vent (DWV) pipe*, and *discharge pipe*. Technically, although all carry waste, only soil pipes carry toilet discharge. All drain systems include one or more vent pipes—open-topped pipes that typically extend up through the roof and allow air into the drain system to prevent suction that would hinder natural drainage (which relies solely on gravity to work). Vent piping is the same material as drain/waste piping.

Pipe sections are connected with fittings (Chapters 24 and 25) that allow piping to make turns and to connect it to fixtures, including sinks, tubs, and toilets. Every type of pipe has its own type and kind of fittings, i.e., copper pipe/copper fittings. Pipe size is almost always described and ordered in terms of its inside diameter—a 1-inch pipe has a 1-inch inside diameter. This is the "nominal" size; it is not meant to be exact. The outside diameter varies with the wall thickness of the pipe material. For example, cast-iron pipe is thicker than copper pipe, so 1-inch cast-iron pipe has a larger outside diameter than 1-inch copper pipe. You don't need to know the outside diameter when choosing pipe, but it's something to keep in mind for projects, such as when a pipe has to fit through a hole in a wall.

Pipe is considered a *male* component and the fittings into which it fits are *female*. Threaded male pipe has threads on the outside; threaded female fittings have threads on the inside. This male-female designation is used to describe all fittings. Fittings that don't have threads are often called *slip* (for plastic fittings, which are glued in place) or *sweat* (for copper fittings, which are soldered in place).

As a general rule, use the same type of pipe and fittings for each piping run or installation. Different plastics don't always bond properly to one another, and joining different metals can lead to corrosion (through a process called electrolytic, or galvanic, action). Where dissimilar materials are joined, you must use a fitting designed for the specific materials and application.

Copper Pipe & Tubing

DESCRIPTION:

Rigid copper pipe for water comes in diameters from ⅛ to 12 inch (measured on the outside diameter, or "O.D."), and of various wall thicknesses known as types K (thick), L (medium), and M (thin), as well as DWV type (thin). Available in rigid 20- or 21-foot lengths with unthreaded ends, 10-foot lengths with

¼" flexible
copper tubing

½" rigid
copper pipe

threaded ends capped for protection, and coils of 45, 60, 100, and 200 feet (types K and L). *Drawn* is hard; *annealed* is soft.

USE:
Hot- and cold-water supply piping, hot-water heating systems, waste piping.

USE TIPS:
Type L is most common for residential use. It can be cut with a hacksaw, but cuts with an inexpensive hand tool called a tubing cutter are easier and much cleaner and straighter. Connections for water piping are usually made with sweat-soldered fittings (page 161) or compression fittings (page 161). Professionals use flare fittings (page 164) for some connections. You can also use push-in fittings (page 162) for water-pipe connections, if allowed by local code. Use only the same thickness (types K, L, or M) in a single contiguous line of plumbing. Flexible copper tubing, commonly ¼ inch, is used for supplying water to refrigerator ice makers.

BUYING TIPS:
Copper remains the gold standard for water piping and is preferred by many plumbers. However, due to its high cost, the skill required to make reliable solder joints, and the challenges of installing rigid pipe runs, it is being replaced by PEX tubing (page 153) in many applications. Copper is very seldom used as drain/waste pipe, due to the cost.

Rigid Plastic Pipe

TYPES:
Polyvinyl chloride (PVC)
Chlorinated polyvinyl chloride (CPVC)
Acrylonitrile-butadiene-styrene (ABS)

DESCRIPTION:
The most common rigid plastic piping used in homes. Sold in 10- and 20-foot lengths and in smaller, precut sizes. Standard diameters used in homes are ½, ¾, 1¼, 1½, 2, 3, and 4 inches. Standard grade for residential use is *Schedule 40*, which refers to the thickness of the pipe wall (*schedule 80* is thicker). Rigid plastic pipe and fittings are permanently joined with solvent cement (page 152). Threaded fittings are also available. There are many color varieties, but PVC is typically white (also commonly gray), CPVC is off-white, and ABS is usually black.

ABS pipe   PVC pipe   CPVC pipe

USE:

PVC:
Drain/waste piping. Code rules vary on other uses. In many areas, PVC is used for underground supply piping between the city water main and the house, and sometimes it is approved for cold-water supply inside houses, though this use is uncommon. It is not approved for hot-water supply. If used outdoors, may require paint or other protection from sunlight, which weakens PVC over time.

CPVC:
Indoor hot- and cold-water piping. Rated for higher temperatures than PVC.

ABS:
Drain/waste piping.

USE TIPS:
Cuts most easily and quickly with a power miter saw. Also can be cut with a ratcheting plastic pipe cutter (scissor-like hand tool), hacksaw, or most wood-cutting saws. Remove burrs from cut ends before joining

pipe to fittings. PVC is a favorite among DIYers because it's cheap and very easy to work with. Also a handy material for crafts and outdoor building projects. Non-plumbing projects can be assembled with or without solvent cement.

Solvent Cement (& Primer)

ALSO KNOWN AS:
Solvent weld, solvent glue, PVC cement.

DESCRIPTION:
Liquid chemical glue sold in small metal containers (two sizes). The container cap is also an applicator and is connected to a metal rod with a fiber "dauber" end for spreading the glue around pipes and inside fittings. Bonds plastic plumbing parts through a chemical fusing process, not conventional adhesion, making a permanent connection. *Primer* is a similar liquid applied to both parts of a joint prior to applying the cement; required for some types of solvent cement. *All-in-one* cement is a primer and cement in one formula.

NOTE:
Use the specific cement and primer intended for the type of pipe; e.g., PVC cement for PVC pipe; ABS cement for ABS pipe. Do not use PVC cement on ABS or vice versa.

USE:
Joining PVC, CPVC, and ABS pipe to fittings of the same material.

USE TIPS:
Solvent cement is easy to use and pretty foolproof, but there are right and wrong ways to use it. Follow the manufacturer's instructions carefully. Pipe must be fully seated inside fittings to create a reliable seal. Hold the pipe and fitting together for 30 seconds while cement bonds; if not held, the pieces can be pushed apart slightly by the cement.

Solvent cements and primers.

PEX Tubing

DESCRIPTION:

Flexible plastic pipe made of cross-linked polyethylene. Sold in long coils of 50 to 500 feet, in standard supply pipe diameters of ¼, ⅜, ½, ¾, and 1 inch. Connections are made with special fittings, with the pipe secured with a metal ring that's crimped with a special hand tool; no soldering or solvent cement required. Also can be joined with compatible push-in fittings (page 162). Tubing can be bent 90° (or more, with a guide fitting)

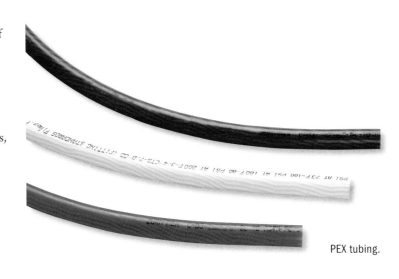

PEX tubing.

so no elbows are needed, as with rigid piping. Can be spliced onto copper, iron, PVC, and CPVC pipe with appropriate transition fittings. Resistant to damage from freezing but not freezeproof; must be protected against freezing, as with other supply piping. Must not be exposed to sunlight or high temperatures.

USE:

Hot- and cold-water supply piping and hot-water heating systems. Commonly used in new construction and remodels as an alternative to copper pipe.

USE TIPS:

PEX is now widely accepted by code authorities for use in homes, but confirm all installation rules and requirements with your local authority.

BUYING TIPS:

Tubing, fittings, and other devices from different manufacturers are not interchangeable; you may void warranties if you mix materials from different manufacturers. Choose the appropriate material type for your application—water supply tubing may not be the same as tubing for heating systems, for example. Some manufacturers offer the same tubing in different colors for distinguishing between hot and cold water, primarily for convenience.

Galvanized Steel Pipe

ALSO KNOWN AS:
Iron pipe, malleable pipe, steel pipe.

DESCRIPTION:
Gray, zinc-treated steel. The zinc (galvanized) treatment, makes the steel rust-resistant if not scratched. Commonly comes in 21-foot lengths, which plumbing stores and larger hardware stores will cut to order, as well as in shorter precut lengths, usually in sections of 6 inches up to 6 feet, threaded on both ends. Pipe diameters range from ⅛ to 6 inches. Common water sizes are ⅜ to 1 inch. Common waste sizes are 1½, 2, and 3 inches. Both ends should be threaded to be screwed into correspondingly threaded fittings; lengths can be threaded on one end only (T.O.E.) if you want.

Galvanized steel pipe.

USE:
Water pipe, waste pipe, and various structural applications, such as fence posts and other vertical supports.

NOTE:
Galvanized pipe cannot be used for gas or steam piping.

BUYING TIPS:
Check to make sure the threads are not damaged before leaving the store. Because galvanized pipes corrode over time, it is often replaced with copper, PEX, CPVC, or PVC piping, depending on the application.

Black Iron Pipe

ALSO KNOWN AS:
B.I. pipe, black pipe.

Black iron pipe.

DESCRIPTION:
Similar to galvanized steel pipe, but not treated for rust resistance. Darker and often more seamless than steel pipe. Slightly greasy to the touch.

USE:
Traditionally used for steam or gas piping. Also popular today for DIY building projects, used as supports for bookshelves and desks, and for light fixtures. The wide, round flange fittings (page 172) are handy for mounting pipe structures to walls, ceilings, and floors.

USE TIPS:
Only black fittings can be used with black iron pipe. Gas and steam piping is best left to a professional plumber. Black pipe is not suitable for water or waste piping.

Cast-Iron Pipe

ALSO KNOWN AS:
Soil pipe, soil stack.

DESCRIPTION:
Very heavy pipe that comes in two weights—*service* and *extra-heavy*. It is commonly sold in lengths of 5 and 10 feet and in diameters of 2, 3, and 4 inches. Two kinds exist. The old, classic kind has a bell hub on one end and a spigot hub (raised end) on the other, but the new kind is plain and known as No-Hub® or *hubless*. Sections of the old kind are joined with a packing of oakum and lead, while the hubless kind is joined with a special hubless fitting (page 163) that is simply tightened down over the joint.

USE:
Waste piping.

USE TIPS:
Only a professional should tackle oakum and lead joints. The new, hubless pipe can be done by the do-it-yourselfer, if allowed by local code, but the pipe is so heavy and hard to handle that is not recommended. It's often easiest to replace damaged sections or entire pipe runs with plastic ABS or PVC pipe. You can splice plastic pipe onto old iron with a hubless fitting. Remove unneeded iron pipe, such as during renovations, by shattering it with a sledgehammer or cutting it into manageable pieces with a reciprocating saw.

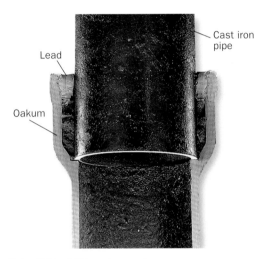

Note: Hubbed fitting shown cut away.

Brass Pipe

DESCRIPTION:
Solid brass, usually sold in unthreaded 12-foot lengths and in all standard sizes. Comes in various weights.

USE:
Water supply and distribution, where resistance to corrosion is the main concern.

USE TIPS:
All threaded connections. Not commonly used in homes.

BUYING TIPS:
More expensive than other types of pipe.

PE Tubing

DESCRIPTION:

Flexible plastic tubing made of polyethylene. PE material is used for many types of tubing, but the most common household types are lightweight black tubing for irrigation systems and 4-inch corrugated pipe for drainage systems. The former comes in ½-, ¾-, and 1-inch diameters and coiled lengths from 100 to 500 feet. It is very thin-walled and easy to cut with a utility knife or tubing cutter. Connections are made with insert fittings (page 163), with or without hose clamps (page 159).

PE tubing.

USE:

STANDARD TUBING:
Lawn-sprinkler systems and drip irrigation systems.

CORRUGATED PIPE:
Landscape drainage systems, French drains, foundation drains.

USE TIPS:

Irrigation tubing is durable and UV-resistant, but its thin walls are easily cut by shovels and the like. Be careful where you dig around sprinkler systems and where you work in the garden around aboveground tubing.

BUYING TIPS:

Buy plenty of "goof plugs" for repairing holes made by mistake when installing drip systems or when you move a branch/drip line to another location on the main tubing.

ABOUT TUBULAR GOODS

Tubular goods are drain pipes used underneath sinks and sometimes bathtubs. They have their own type of joining system, using slip nuts, and are easy to work with.

Tubular Goods

ALSO KNOWN AS:

Drainage fittings, drain pipes, drain kits, slip-joint pipe, sink drains.

DESCRIPTION:

Specialty pipes and fittings that make up a drain assembly under a sink. Piping is made of plastic or chromed brass, and even chromed plastic. Pipes for kitchen sinks are usually 1½ inches in diameter; bathroom sinks (lavatory) usually 1¼ inches. Typically held together and made watertight by *slip-joints*, consisting of slip nuts and plastic or rubber washers, though some tailpieces that attach to sink strainers have threaded ends. Washers may be called *cut sj washers*.

The main parts of a sink drain assembly include the *tailpiece*, a vertical pipe that connects to the sink drain assembly, may also include the assembly that mounts to both sides of the sink basin, and contains a sink strainer (kitchen) or the stopper assembly (bathroom). The *P-trap*, also called J-bend, a short drain piece shaped like the letter J, connects to the tailpiece. And the *trap arm*, a straight drain piece with a 90° bend at one end, attaches to drain pipe in wall. Kitchen sinks with two basins (and some double bathroom sinks) also have an additional drain pipe with a 90° bend (similar to a trap arm) and a *waste tee*, which connects the additional drain pipe to the main drain assembly.

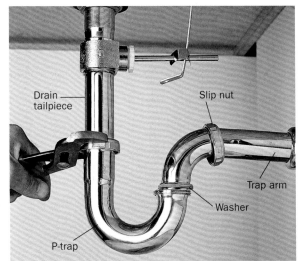

Corrugated flexible drain is plastic pipe that can be bent as needed to accommodate drain parts that are out of alignment. Although these pipes are widely available, they are not allowed by code in most areas because they collect solid waste in the corrugation folds and are prone to clogging; they never should be used in place of a P-trap.

USE:
To route waste water from a sink, disposer, or tub to other drain pipes. P-traps retain water in their bends to provide a barrier against sewer odors and vermin.

USE TIPS:
Most slip nuts can simply be hand-tightened. If necessary, you can loosen or tighten a slip nut with tongue-and-groove pliers, but do so carefully, as the nuts and drain parts are relatively weak. After assembly, run lots of water down the sink and check all slip-joints for leaks. Usually aligning the pipes and tightening the slip nuts a bit stops any leaking.

BUYING TIPS:
Plain plastic is the cheapest material, but not the best looking. If the lines will be out of sight, plastic is fine. If it's visible, chromed brass is recommended over chromed plastic. Some brands come with slip fittings and others do not; be sure to check before leaving the store. Some P-traps include a cleanout plug at the bottom of the bend. These come in handy occasionally, but usually it's best to remove the trap entirely for a thorough cleaning of the trap and the sink tailpiece.

Water Supply Tubes

ALSO KNOWN AS:
Faucet supply lines, water connectors, toilet supply tube, supply hose.

DESCRIPTION:

Short ⅜-inch-diameter tubes in common lengths of 8 to 24 inches
but are available up to 96 inches. Made of braided steel,
copper, chromed copper or brass, corrugated copper, or vinyl
mesh. Most types have ends designed for compression fittings;
some with two female ends with nuts, some with one female
and one male, etc.

USE:

Makes the connection between the water supply valve
(page 186) and a sink faucet, toilet, dishwasher, ice maker,
or other fixtures.

USE TIPS:

Braided steel and vinyl mesh are highly flexible and the
easiest to use. Steel (which has a core of vinyl and/or nylon)
is more durable than vinyl mesh, which is primarily used for
kitchen sink sprayers. Copper tubing can be kinked easily
(making it highly prone to leaks) and must be cut to the proper length and bent carefully.

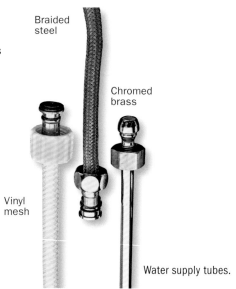

Braided steel

Chromed brass

Vinyl mesh

Water supply tubes.

BUYING TIPS:

Check the size of the fittings/nuts at *both* ends of the tubing; they may not be the same—for example, a tube
may be sized for a ½-inch connection at one end and a ⅜-inch connection at the other. Choose a length
of flexible tubing that allows for some slack; you don't want to pull the tubing tight between connections.
Too long is better than too short, because you can coil the excess.

Flexible Gas Hose

ALSO KNOWN AS:

Gas range or dryer connector, gas supply tubing.

DESCRIPTION:

Stainless steel, either corrugated (CSST) or steel-wire hose, with or without a PVC coating, with brass hex fittings
on the ends. Comes in a range of lengths from 6 to 12 inches in ½- or ¾-inch diameters. Modern appliances have ½-
inch fittings, but typical supply lines are ¾ inch. Adapters for reducing the connection are available with the hose.

USE:

Connects gas supply line to kitchen gas stove, gas clothes dryer, outdoor grill, or gas water heater.

USE TIPS:

Use plenty of pipe dope (page 174)—not tape—and care. Make sure no kinks are in the line. Test completed
connections by brushing with soapy water and examining connection for bubbles.

Pipe-Hanging Tape

ALSO KNOWN AS:

Hanger strap, pipe hanger, band iron, band clamp.

DESCRIPTION:

Steel, copper, or plastic band with holes at regular intervals, sold in coils.

USE:

Suspending pipes of all sizes from walls and ceilings, using screws.

USE TIPS:

On copper pipe, use only copper tape, not steel.

Pipe-hanging tape.

Pipe Strap & Tube Strap

DESCRIPTION:

Pipe strap is a U-shaped piece of plastic or galvanized steel with two holes in flanges; tube strap is similar but made of copper for copper tubing. A *suspension clamp* is a split ring with two ears for suspending pipe from framing.

USE:

Screwed or nailed to wood framing or other structure to secure pipe, typically used with water pipe. Helps keep pipe from rubbing or banging against framing when it moves.

Hose Clamp

DESCRIPTION:

Stainless-steel band with notches and a gear mechanism that tightens and loosens the band. Gear is driven with a $5/16$-inch socket wrench or nut driver, or a flathead screwdriver. Another type is a *spring-type clamp*, made of thick metal wire and commonly used on car radiator hoses and clothes dryer vents; these are not suitable for connections on water-supply piping.

USE:

To apply even pressure around pipe or hose; in particular to clamp a hose or a gasket onto a tube or pipe. Also used with insert fittings (page 163).

USE TIPS:

Don't overtighten. If you have many to do, use a $5/16$-inch nut driver or a T-handle torque wrench.

Hose clamp.

CHAPTER 24

FITTINGS

ABOUT FITTINGS

Fittings are devices that allow plumbing pipes to be joined together, change direction, or connect to fixtures. For each kind of pipe and tubing there are fittings made of the same material, wall thickness, and sizes. Exceptions include the metal fittings used with PEX and other plastic pipe, as well as neoprene couplings used with cast-iron pipe. Pages 160 to 165 cover the basic types of fitting—such as threaded or soldered. Pages 166 to 173 discuss the most common shapes or forms of fittings, such as elbows and tees. Most fittings come in more than one type.

A word on terminology: the opening of a fitting may be called a *socket*, *outlet*, or *port*. *Socket* is the logical term for female openings, *outlet* for male, but there are no official rules about this usage.

ABOUT THREADED FITTINGS

Threaded fittings are often described by a coding system that dates back to the days when all threaded pipe was iron or steel. The coding refers to the thread type. Metal pipe and fittings are either *MPT* (also *MIPT*), for Male Iron Pipe Thread, or *FPT* (also *FIPT*), for Female Iron Pipe Thread. A pipe with an MPT-threaded end fits an FPT fitting.

Rigid plastic parts follow a different system. They may be labeled *NPT*, for National Pipe Thread, or *NIPT*, for National Iron Pipe Thread, which means the same thing (never mind that plastic pipe has nothing to do with iron). MPT/FPT and NPT threads are not compatible. A third threading system is *hose thread*, which fits garden hoses and sillcocks; this threading is not compatible with either MPT/FPT or NPT. If you're using pipe and fittings of the same material, chances are they will have compatible threads. But if you mix materials, make sure the threads are the same type, or use an adapter or coupling that has the right threads for each piece.

Threaded Fitting

DESCRIPTION:

The most common type of fitting, with male (exterior) or female (interior) threads at each opening. Comes in most materials and sizes. Fittings may have only threaded sockets or outlets (sometimes called adapters; see page 164), or they may have unthreaded openings as well as threaded.

USE:

Connecting water supply, waste, steam, and gas piping systems in all kinds of threaded pipe.

USE TIPS:

Use plenty of pipe dope (page 174) or thread seal tape (page 175) on the threads of metal pipes to prevent leaks and reduce corrosion.

Threaded nipple.

Sweat-Soldered Fitting

ALSO KNOWN AS:

Copper fitting (incorrect), sweats.

DESCRIPTION:

Smooth-ended (no threads) copper pipe fitting with a slightly enlarged end that receives copper pipe.

Copper sweat fitting.

USE:

Connecting copper pipe or tubing.

USE TIPS:

Ensure that fittings are clean before soldering and that plenty of flux (page 176) is used. Soldering *copper pipe joints* is not all that difficult, but the technique must be mastered before you attempt it on water supply piping, lest you end up with leaks hidden behind walls, etc. Do not use lead solder on water supply lines.

BUYING TIPS:

Also available with solder pre-applied.

Compression Fitting

DESCRIPTION:

Two-piece copper or plastic device that uses a nut and a metal or plastic ring on the end of a pipe that is inserted into a fitting. As the nut is tightened the ring presses into the fitting and the pipe, making a watertight seal.

USE:

Connecting water supply tubes, fittings, and valves supplying fixtures or wherever one wants to avoid using sweat fittings. A *compression union* splices the ends of two pipes together. Compression fittings are removable and are commonly used on water supply valves and tubing for faucets, toilets, and other fixtures where the connections are easily accessible. They are not recommended for joints in enclosed cavities, such as inside walls and floors, where leaks can go unnoticed for long periods.

BUYING TIPS:

The small rings and nuts can be bought individually in case one is lost.

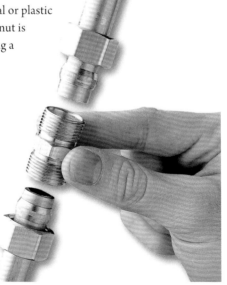

Compression fitting.

Push-In Fitting

ALSO KNOWN AS:

SharkBite® (brand name).

DESCRIPTION:

Metal fitting that works by simply pushing the pipe end about 1 inch into the fitting port. Contains internal stainless-steel teeth that hold the pipe firmly and a plastic washer that creates a watertight seal. Pipe end can be removed from fitting with a small, plastic, horseshoe-shaped disconnect tool, by pressing the tool against a plastic sleeve around the pipe. Wide range of fittings available, as well as valves and couplings. Expensive compared to standard fittings, but extremely handy, particularly where soldering copper is difficult or when making quick repairs.

USE:

Joints for copper, PEX, PVC, and CPVC supply pipe only. Designed for permanent watertight connections, but must be installed according to manufacturer's directions.

USE TIPS:

Confirm use and installation requirements with the local building code authority. May not be allowed in all areas or for some concealed connections (joints hidden behind drywall, etc.).

Push-in fitting and disconnect tools.

Solvent-Welded Fittings

ALSO KNOWN AS:
Slip fittings, glued fittings, cemented fittings.

DESCRIPTION:
Plastic fittings with slightly enlarged, threadless sockets designed for use with solvent cement (page 152). Called *slip fittings* in the trade. They look similar to copper sweat-soldered fittings (page 161). Considered the best joining method for plastic pipe and fittings. "Slip" may refer to an individual socket on a fitting; a fitting with one slip socket and one threaded socket is commonly designated as "slip x thread" or "slip-by-thread."

USE:
Rigid plastic plumbing connections.

PVC slip fitting.

Insert Fitting

ALSO KNOWN AS:
Barbed fitting, insert.

DESCRIPTION:
Ridged plastic or metal piece that is inserted into the end of flexible plastic pipe and typically clamped in place with a stainless-steel hose-type clamp (page 159). Made of brass, nylon, polypropylene, or polystyrene.

USE:
Connecting flexible plastic pipe to other pieces or fittings, including to standard female threads. Common on lawn sprinkler systems.

Insert fitting.

Hubless Fitting

ALSO KNOWN AS:
No-Hub®, no-hub clamp, no-hub band, banded coupling.

DESCRIPTION:
A neoprene (black rubber) sleeve, or gasket, covered by a corrugated metal sleeve, or *clamp band*, with hose-type clamps on each end.

USE:

Connecting hubless or No-Hub® cast iron pipe sections and fittings. Also cast iron to plastic.

USE TIPS:

Clamp nuts can be tightened down with a small wrench, screwdriver, a $5/16$-inch nut driver, or a special tool called a T-handle, or No-Hub® torque wrench. The T-handle contains an internal mechanism that prevents overtightening and speeds the job.

3" no-hub neoprene coupling

Hubless fitting.

Flare Fitting

ALSO KNOWN AS:

S.A.E. flare.

DESCRIPTION:

Similar to a compression fitting (above) but with an end that is expanded, or flared, to fit against the beveled end of the fitting.

USE:

Used usually with flexible copper pipe, mostly for refrigeration and oil heating systems and small appliance lines. Similar to *sweat-soldered fittings* but installed without using a torch, which can be important in areas where fire would be a risk. Prohibited by some codes.

USE TIPS:

Leave flare fittings to professionals. Any plumbing repairs or installations you make won't require flare fittings, and if they're needed for refrigeration/heating equipment, that's strictly professional territory.

Adapter

ALSO KNOWN AS:

Transition fitting.

DESCRIPTION:

Common term for virtually anything that helps connect two normally incompatible things—hoses to pipes, metal to plastic, MPT/FPT to NPT threads, or whatever. When describing fittings, though, it is a type of coupling or union with a different type of joining method on each end, e.g., thread x sweat, thread x slip, etc.

Dielectric union fitting.

TYPES:

TRANSITION UNION ADAPTER:

Special fitting designed to compensate for thermal differences in expansion and contraction between metal and plastic pipe.

DIELECTRIC ADAPTER:

For connecting galvanized to copper.

USE:

TRANSITION UNION:

Allows you to connect different kinds of pipe, such as plastic to galvanized, or copper to plastic, etc.

DIELECTRIC FITTING:

Allows connecting dissimilar metals and prevents destructive *galvanic* or *electrolytic* action, a major cause of rust and corrosion. Typically used under faucets where copper pipe connects with galvanized. Suitable for both water supply and waste lines.

Flexible Coupling

ALSO KNOWN AS:

Fernco Coupling (brand name).

DESCRIPTION:

Length of soft plastic (elastomeric PVC or polyurethane) that slips over the outside ends of waste pipe and is secured by hose clamps. Heavier yet more flexible than hubless fittings (page 163). Comes in a variety of dimensions and shapes as a reducer coupling (page 171).

USE:

Waste lines only, but fits over any kind of pipe. Especially useful where precise alignment is not possible, or where some flexibility is needed and where connecting two pipes of different diameters. A "forgiving" fitting.

ABOUT FITTING SHAPES & FORMS

These shapes, or forms, are made in all the various pipe materials, but regardless of the material, they resemble one another (each photo shows just a specific type and material). The nomenclature is the same.

Elbow

TYPES:

90° elbow

45° elbow

Drop-ear elbow

Side-outlet elbow

Sweep elbow

Street elbow

Closet bend

ALSO KNOWN AS:

Ell, L, S.O. ell (side-outlet ell).

NOTE:

Similar to and easily confused with cast-iron fittings ¼ bend (90°) and ⅛ bend (45°).

DESCRIPTION:

Simple fitting that makes a right-angle (90°) or 45° bend. May be threaded or unthreaded, or both. Also available in insert (barbed) fittings. Common specialty types include:

DROP-EAR:

Also known as *drop ells*, ears, or flanges, for attaching to a wall.

SIDE-OUTLET:

Essentially an elbow with an additional socket on one side. Useful in corners of construction or for making railings or fences.

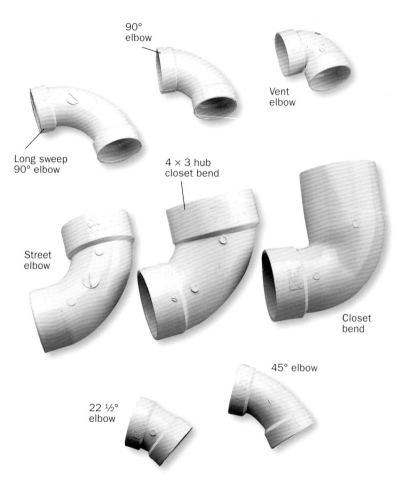

Long sweep 90° elbow

90° elbow

Vent elbow

4 × 3 hub closet bend

Street elbow

Closet bend

22 ½° elbow

45° elbow

PVC elbows (for drain-waste-vent runs; supply elbows shown on page 168).

SWEEP:

Similar to an elbow in that it consists of two openings at 90° or 45° to each other. Comes in "long" version as well as normal to create a longer curve to fit different situations and/or to create a gentler change in direction. If replacing an existing piece of plumbing, be sure to measure the sweep to see if it is "long" or normal.

STREET:

90° or 45° elbow with a male outlet on one end and female socket on the other (or male/female threads for metal pipe). Joins pipes at corners with the male end going into a fitting or valve.

CLOSET BEND:

Large elbow that connects the toilet flange (below the base of the toilet; see page 195) to the toilet waste pipe.

USE:

Joins pipes for corners at a 90° or 45° angle. Used on all types of plumbing runs: supply, waste, vent, irrigation, etc.

Tee

ALSO KNOWN AS:

T, T-fitting, straight tee, reducing tee, sanitary tee.

DESCRIPTION:

Three openings, two in a line and one on the side, in a T shape. *Straight tees* have the same size openings; *reducing tees* have one opening of a different size. *Sanitary tees*, used in waste lines, have a curved branch that is slightly offset, for a cleanout plug, and a smooth inside. A *cross* is a T-fitting with four outlets forming a cross shape.

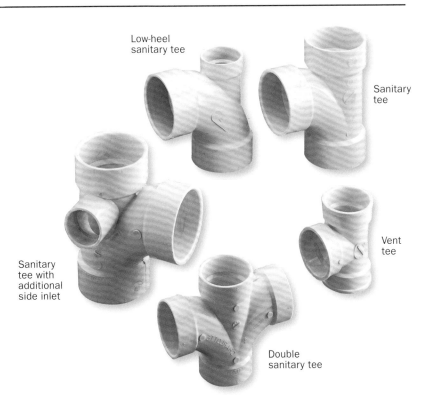

Low-heel sanitary tee

Sanitary tee

Sanitary tee with additional side inlet

Vent tee

Double sanitary tee

PVC tees (for drain-waste-vent runs; supply tees shown on page 166).

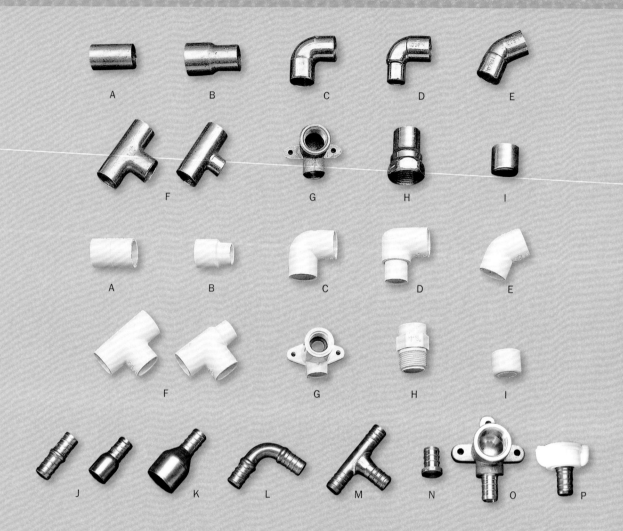

Water supply fittings are available for copper (top), CPVC plastic (center), and PEX (bottom). Fittings for copper and CPVC are available in many shapes, including unions (A), reducers (B), 90° elbows (C), reducing elbows (D), 45° elbows (E), tee fittings (F), drop-ear elbows (G), threaded adapters (H), and caps (I). Common PEX fittings (bottom) include unions (J), PEX-to-copper unions (K), 90° elbows (L), tee fittings (M), plugs (N), drop-ear elbows (O), and threaded adapters (P). Easy-to-install push-in fittings are also available.

USE:

Connecting three pipes. *Sanitary tees* are for waste lines where lack of obstruction is important.

BUYING TIPS:

When ordering a reducing tee, specify the lateral, or horizontal, dimensions first, followed by the vertical branch. Keep the letter T in mind. For example, 1 x 1 x 1½ inches. Be sure to mention the use you have in mind, as there is some variety in sanitary tees.

Wye

ALSO KNOWN AS:

Y-fitting, Y brand, reducing Y.

DESCRIPTION:

Similar to at tee but with the side outlet set at an angle to the line of the other two outlets. The side outlet can be the same size as the other two or, in the case of a *reducing wye*, can be smaller.

USE:

Bringing together two pipes from similar directions; typically used for drain-waste-vent lines.

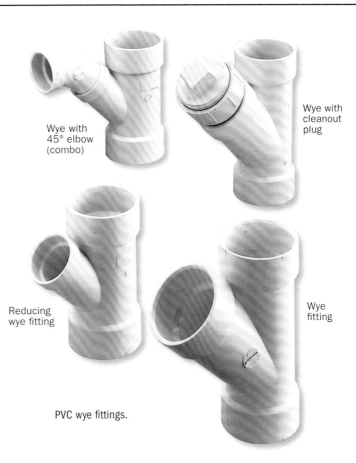

Wye with 45° elbow (combo)

Wye with cleanout plug

Reducing wye fitting

Wye fitting

PVC wye fittings.

Plug

ALSO KNOWN AS:
Hex head plug, square head plug, round head plug, cleanout plug.

DESCRIPTION:
A short, solid piece with male threads and a hexagonal, square, or round head. A *cleanout plug* has a square protrusion in the middle for a wrench to grab.

USE:
Seals female ends of fittings or valves and the like. Cleanout plugs allow access into pipe for cleaning with a plumbing snake or sewer auger; commonly installed into a wye fitting (page 169).

Nipple

ALSO KNOWN AS:
Close (if threads from each end of a straight nipple meet or almost meet in the middle), straight nipple.

DESCRIPTION:
Any piece of pipe that is less than 12 inches and male threaded on both ends. Generally stocked in lengths from *close* (minimum) to 12 inches; lengths beyond this are usually considered *cut pipe* and are available in 6-inch increments. *Reducing nipple* has a different diameter on each end.

USE:
Links longer pipe sections where the final "fit" is being made, such as the span between two fittings in a run of pipe. Reducing nipple connects different sizes of pipe in place of a bushing (page 172) and coupling (page 171) combination. Provides a smoother, neater connection.

Cap

ALSO KNOWN AS:
End, end cap.

DESCRIPTION:
A short, closed end piece with a threaded or unthreaded (slip) female socket.

Cap.

USE:
Seals male end of pipe at the end of a run or when a fitting or valve has been removed.

Coupling, Reducing Coupling

ALSO KNOWN AS:
Straight coupling, reducing bell (reducing coupling), reducer (reducing coupling).

DESCRIPTION:
Short length of pipe with slip sockets or female threads, generally no longer than the threaded area itself. Reducing couplings have two different-sized openings. An odd cousin is the *extension coupling*, which has female threads on one end and male on the other.

Reducing coupling.

USE:
Connects lengths of pipe that are not intended to be disconnected. A *reducing coupling* connects pipes of different diameters. Can also be used in combination with bushings (page 172) when there are large differences in pipe diameters. An *extension coupling* extends the length of a pipe just an inch or two, which is less than is possible with a regular coupling; this is commonly used with radiators after new, thicker floors have been installed.

Coupling.

BUYING TIPS:
When buying a reducing coupling state the larger dimension—2 × 1½ inches, etc.

Dresser Coupling

ALSO KNOWN AS:
Mender coupler, slip fitting, "no-thread" fitting, mender dresser.

DESCRIPTION:
A fitting with a short length of pipe or a nipple in the center and a compression fitting on each end. Available in copper, steel, and plastic.

USE:
Slips onto unthreaded pipe ends to make a convenient connection, often used to cover a leaking section (after the pipe has been cut through) or where a very slight flexibility is needed.

USE TIPS:
May be used on supply or waste lines. Helpful where threading is impossible, such as when replacing a damaged section.

Flange

ALSO KNOWN AS:
Floor flange.

DESCRIPTION:
Round, female-threaded fitting that can take pipe up to 2 inches, surrounded by flat flange with holes that permit attaching to a floor or a wall with screws or bolts.

USE:
Often a nonplumbing use, such as making a railing or table or other furniture. Pipe just screws into the flange and is relatively solid.

Hex Bushing, Flush Bushing

ALSO KNOWN AS:
Bushing.

DESCRIPTION:
Short plug (threaded, with hexagonal top) or nipple (flush)-type piece with female threads inside.

USE:
Joining pipe of dissimilar size. Bushings fit inside other fittings, especially couplings, and can be combined to reduce pipe as required.

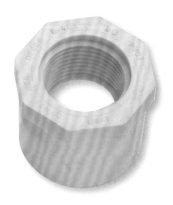

Hex bushing.

Pipe Repair Coupling

DESCRIPTION:
Short length of pipe with a push-in fitting (page 162) at each end.

USE:
Repairing burst or otherwise damaged water pipe where damaged area is no more than 2 inches long. After damaged area is cut out, coupling is slipped onto one pipe, and then slipped back to attach to the other pipe end, bridging the gap. Works on copper and CPVC water pipe.

Union

ALSO KNOWN AS:

Ground joint union.

DESCRIPTION:

Splicing device with three threaded nuts. Its two halves are separated and screwed (metal pipe) or solvent-welded (plastic pipe) onto the ends of the pipes to be joined, then the larger, central hex nut is tightened down to join them.

USE:

Connecting pipe sections of similar size that are expected to be disassembled or that are being fit into a position between two fixed pipes. Commonly used with gas piping, to allow for future disassembly, and with PVC piping for pools and spas, allowing the removal of inline heaters, filter or motor housings, etc.

PVC Union.

CHAPTER 25

JOINT COMPOUNDS & SEALANTS

Pipe Joint Compound

ALSO KNOWN AS:

Pipe dope, thread sealant.

NOTE:

Do not confuse with drywall joint compound (page 130), which is a totally different material. Different types of compound are available for pipes carrying oils and gases.

DESCRIPTION:

Thick, oily paste applied to pipe threads before assembly. Sold in small tube and canisters; the latter usually include an applicator brush connected to the canister lid.

USE:

Helps prevent leaks and makes for easier disassembly; also helps prevent corrosion of exposed threads where the zinc coating has been removed during the threading process.

USE TIP:

Use gloves—some kinds of pipe dopes are extremely difficult to clean off of hands. Apply liberally.

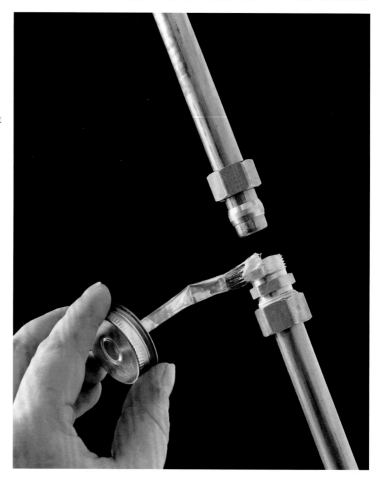

Pipe joint compound (in use).

Works well, but thread seal tape (page 175) is a neater and faster option for the same job.

Thread Seal Tape

ALSO KNOWN AS:
Pipe thread tape, pipe thread sealant tape, Teflon® tape (brand name).

DESCRIPTION:
Thin, stretchy, white tape sold in rolls from ¼ to ¾ inch wide and in various lengths. Most commonly called "Teflon tape" but is not made from the trademarked material Teflon®. *Gas-rated* or *fuel-line* versions (made with PTFE polymer) are designed for gas piping connections.

USE:
Applied to pipe threads before assembly; same as pipe joint compound (page 174). Standard version is not for use on gas pipes.

Thread seal tape.

USE TIP:
Try to keep the tape flat and smooth as you wrap it around the threads, always wrapping in the same direction as the nut or fitting will tighten onto the threads (this is usually clockwise when viewed from the end of the pipe, unless the treads are reverse threads). How much to wrap depends on the tape thickness and the threads; three to five wraps is common.

Epoxy Repair Putty

ALSO KNOWN AS:
Epoxy repair material, epoxy.

DESCRIPTION:
Two-part putty material mixed together just before use. May be a long package resembling a candy bar, or a tube, or a small package resembling a packet of chewing gum. You break off as much as you need of this clay-like substance and massage it a bit, mixing the two parts together.

USE:
Repairs small leaks in drain pipes. Not recommended for repairs on water supply or other pressurized plumbing runs.

USE TIP:

While epoxy cannot be depended on 100 percent to stop a leak, it may work for years. Some kinds work even when applied to a wet pipe.

Solder

DESCRIPTION:

Soft, silver-colored wire sold on a small reel; 95-5 solder is the most common type, made of 95 percent tin and no lead.

USE:

Used in sweat-soldering of copper pipe joints.

USE TIP:

Parts to be soldered must be very clean.

BUYING TIPS:

The old-fashioned kind with lead was outlawed nationally in 1986; use 95-5. If you can't find 95-5 at your hardware store, try a plumbing supply store.

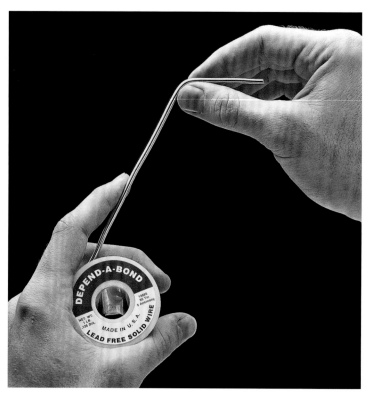

Solder.

Flux

ALSO KNOWN AS:

Soldering paste, solder flux.

DESCRIPTION:

Jelly-like paste. Removes oxidation and other impurities from soldered joints in copper pipe and fittings. Sold in round tins and small plastic tubs.

USE:

To ensure proper fusion of solder to copper sweat-solder joints.

USE TIP:

Clean copper pipe and fittings with a copper fitting cleaning brush, a small tool with a wire handle and a cylindrical black-bristle brush on the end. A *combination brush* has ½- and ¾-inch brushes on either end. Apply a thin coating of flux to the pipe and fitting with a flux brush, a small, metal-handled brush, about 6 inches long, with short bristles.

BUYING TIPS:

Use the *noncorrosive* type, sometimes called *self-cleaning* or *nonacid* type.

Plumber's Putty

DESCRIPTION:

Soft, tan-colored putty that can be rolled by hand into long ropes or beads of any diameter. Sold in small plastic tubs.

USE:

Applied to sink rims, drain plugs, and faucets before installation to ensure a watertight seal. Commonly used under the bases of faucets (when silicone caulk is not used) and around flanges of drain fittings. Easier to remove in the future than caulk.

USE TIP:

Remove all old putty before applying fresh material. Create an even, continuous seal around the item, in a similar manner to applying a bead of caulk. Excess putty will ooze out when the item is tightened into place; simply wipe off excess with a rag.

Plumber's putty (in use).

Stem Packing

ALSO KNOWN AS:

Faucet packing, valve packing, packing, gasket rope, plumber's twine.

DESCRIPTION:

Graphite or Teflon®-impregnated string.

USE:

Wrapped around valve stems (typically under packing nuts) to prevent leaks.

Stem packing.

USE TIP:

If a slow leak at a handle stem cannot be stopped by tightening the nut, just back it off and add more packing—but first make sure the water is off!

Gasket

DESCRIPTION:

A generic term for soft material that fits between two hard items in order to make a seal. It may be made of rubber, plastic, or strong paper and is shaped for each particular use.

USE:

Seals joints in fittings, between parts of valves, and so on.

BUYING TIPS:

Formed gaskets as well as sheets for making your own are available. In some low-pressure cases, you can form your own small gasket in between parts of leaking radiator valves and the like by using a liquid (sold in tubes) made for that purpose.

Oakum

DESCRIPTION:

Short lengths of shredded rope or hemp fiber, sold dry or tarred (oiled). White oakum has a thin, woven coating and is impregnated with a type of cement powder.

USE:

Originally used primarily for sealing old-fashioned hub-and-spigot cast iron waste pipe along with molten lead, but useful for packing any kind of large gap. For example, it could be stuffed into a crack and used as a base for caulking. White oakum, which has dry cement in it, swells when brought into contact with water. Interestingly, oakum and tar were the traditional materials used to caulk the planks of ancient ships' hulls.

USE TIP:

Wear gloves to avoid a nasty cleanup job.

CHAPTER 26

FAUCETS & FAUCET PARTS

ABOUT FAUCETS

Kitchen sink, laundry, and lavatory (bathroom) faucets come in a tremendous array of styles and colors. Some have two handles, some have one, and there are many different finish options—chrome, bronze, nickel, stainless steel, even bare copper.

Most of these options are for aesthetics or usability, but if you're buying a new faucet for an existing sink, you need one that fits the predrilled holes in the sink. Pay attention to the number of holes and the center-to-center, or "centers," dimension—the distance between the center of one handle and the center of the other. Kitchen sinks usually have 8-inch centers but may be 6 inches. Lavatory faucets are usually 4 inches apart but can be 8 inches (sometimes called "widespread"). *Wall-mounted* lavatory (bathroom) faucets are usually on 4¼-inch centers but may be 6 inches. There are also *single-hole* faucets that mount into a single hole in the sink or countertop.

If you're repairing a faucet, always take the old parts into the store, or at least write down the brand and model name of the faucet. When disassembling a faucet, lay out the parts in the order and orientation (right side up) of their assembly. It's all too easy to forget where and how all those foreign-looking parts go back together.

Compression Faucet

ALSO KNOWN AS:
Basin faucet (lavatory).

DESCRIPTION:
Typically older-style faucet that has a threaded *stem* (also called a *spindle* or *valve*) with a rubber washer on the end that presses against the *faucet seat*, a donut-

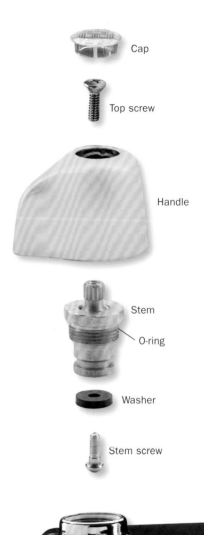

Cap

Top screw

Handle

Stem

O-ring

Washer

Stem screw

Faucet base

Compression faucet.

shaped nut with a hexagonal hole in its center, where the water emerges from the supply pipe. The spindle may have an O-ring that prevents leaking around the handle.

USE:

Controls water flow into basins or sinks.

USE TIPS:

Leaks at the spout are usually due to a worn washer or a pitted, corroded seat. Leaks around the base of the handle indicate a worn O-ring. Replace a stem if it sticks or has rough action due to corrosion. If washers wear out quickly, replace the seat, if possible. Remove the seat with a faucet seat wrench. If it's not removable, smooth the seat with a faucet seat reamer.

BUYING TIPS:

Replacement stems may be sold as "hot" or "cold," with threads corresponding to the way a handle is turned to open or close the faucet. Beveled washers are usually better for repair than flat ones, as they seal better if the seat is worn and pitted. Neoprene is better than rubber.

Washerless Faucet

DESCRIPTION:

Most faucets these days are washerless, which simply means they don't have spindles or stems that move up and down to press a washer against a seat. Instead, washerless faucets have a cartridge with an internal spindle that rotates to open and close the water flow.

USE:

Controls water flow into sinks and basins; includes single- and double-handled models.

USE TIPS:

If a cartridge goes bad, you must replace the entire piece with an identical match. More commonly, leaks are due to a worn O-ring; bring the old O-ring to the store for an exact match (cheap repair!).

Handle

Setscrew

Stem screw

Retaining nut

Cartridge

Faucet base

Washerless faucet.

BUYING TIPS:

Washerless faucets tend to have fewer leaks than compression faucets and are easier to repair when they do have problems. Some models require a special device to remove the cartridge. It is included in the package and should be saved for the next repair.

Ball Faucet

DESCRIPTION:

Type of washerless faucet with a ball that fits into a faucet body that has three holes—a hot inlet, a cold inlet, and an outlet. Depending on the ball's position, outlet water is hot, cold, or somewhere in between. Inlet holes are sealed with little rubber cups, called *valve seats*, pressed against the ball with tiny metal springs.

USE:

Controls water flow into sinks and basins; typically single-handled kitchen faucets.

USE TIPS:

If water drips from the spout, replace the valve seats and springs (sold in sets of two or more). If water leaks from the faucet base/base of spout, replace the O-rings around the faucet body.

Aerator

ALSO KNOWN AS:

Spray diffuser.

DESCRIPTION:

Small, barrel-like metal or plastic part that screws onto the end of a faucet spout with either inside or outside threads. Has a fine screen inside that diffuses the water and introduces air. Made in a variety of sizes and types.

Ball faucet.

USE:

Makes the stream of water coming from a faucet spout smooth and prevents splashing. Also controls flow of water.

USE TIPS:

Unscrew occasionally and clean debris from screen. If it doesn't unscrew by hand, use tongue-and-groove pliers with a rag to protect the chrome finish of the aerator. Soak the aerator overnight in vinegar to dissolve mineral deposits.

Aerator.

BUYING TIPS:

Universal aerators are available that fit most faucets. Low-flow aerators reduce water use; they're a good idea for bathrooms, where the water tends to be left running, but not so great in the kitchen, where high flow is desirable for filling pots and sink basins.

Lavatory Faucet Handle

ALSO KNOWN AS:

Faucet handle.

DESCRIPTION:

Plastic or metal piece that attaches to faucet stem. Available in an almost infinite number of shapes and styles.

USE:

To open and close faucet.

USE TIPS:

On some handles, the screws that hold the handle on the stem are concealed under a decorative cap, often marked "Hot" or "Cold." These must be pried up to gain access to the screws.

BUYING TIPS:

For the best fit, buy a duplicate replacement handle. Failing this, buy a *universal handle*. Types with two setscrews are more secure but may still slip and damage the stem.

Bathtub & Shower Faucets

DESCRIPTION:

A variety of types: three-valve faucets have hot- and cold-water faucets with another faucet in the middle for diverting water to the shower. Two-valve faucets have hot-and cold-water faucets with a lift-up device on the tub spout for diverting the water to the shower. Two-valve shower fittings have hot- and cold-water faucets

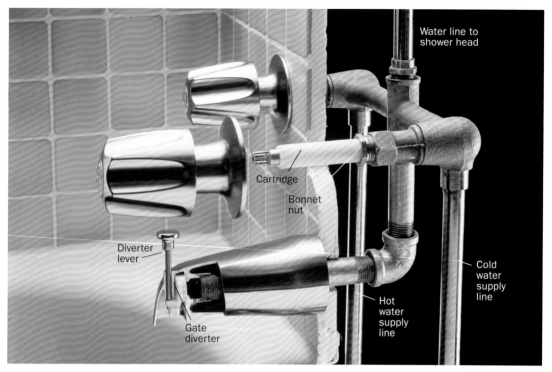

Two-handled washerless tub faucet.

only. Two-valve tub fillers have faucets that fill the tub only. Single-control faucets have one lever that controls the flow and mix of hot and cold water.

The standard center-to-center measurement on tub faucets is 8 inches, though 6- and 11-inch centers are also used. The center measurement on old-style, free-standing tubs with exposed plumbing is 3½ inches. Tub faucets are available in chrome-plated brass or plastic, pot metal, and plain plastic.

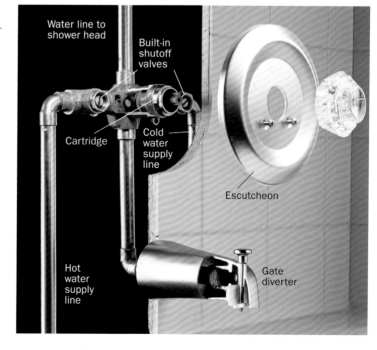

Single-handle washerless tub faucet.

USE:

Controlling water flow and temperature in a shower or bathtub.

USE TIPS:

Older faucets are typically compression-style, while contemporary models typically have cartridges (washerless), as with today's sink faucets. To remove the stem (on compression faucets) or cartridge (on washerless faucets) after the handle is removed, you may need to remove a bonnet nut with a deep-throat socket wrench.

BUYING TIPS:

Replacement parts are the same as those for sink and lavatory faucets.

Sillcock

ALSO KNOWN AS:

Hose bib, spigot, male hose faucet, outdoor faucet.

DESCRIPTION:

Outdoor faucet with a mounting flange for anchoring to an exterior wall and a male-threaded spout for connecting to hoses (a "plain" faucet has no threads). A *frost-proof* sillcock has a pipe that extends 18 inches or so into the house, ending with a valve where the water is shut off. The remaining water in the extension pipe runs out through the spout so there's no water that can freeze at the exposed end of the faucet.

USE:

Exterior water supply, especially to hoses.

USE TIPS:

Many sillcocks are connected to the water supply pipe with a threaded fitting and can be unscrewed for replacement. Frost-proof sillcocks are recommended in areas with freezing winters. These can be installed with compression fittings (page 161) or push-in fittings (page 162) if allowed by local code. Leaks can be repaired the same ways as with other faucets.

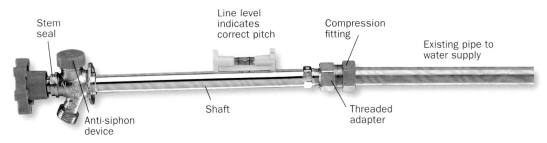

Frost-proof sillcock.

CHAPTER 27

VALVES

|||||||||||||||||||||||||||||||||||||||||||||||||||||||||||||||||||||||||||||||||||||||||||||||||||||||||||

ABOUT VALVES

Valves, like faucets, control the flow of water or steam, but they are stronger and have more specialized characteristics than faucets. Valves and sillcocks are found on plumbing pipes; faucets are simply valves that are used on fixtures such as sinks. Valves are made in all the sizes and types that pipe is made and in most of those materials as well, although cast brass is most common. Installation types—the way in which the valve is joined to the pipe or fitting—include threaded, compression, solvent-weld, push-in, and sweat (soldered).

Water Supply Valve

ALSO KNOWN AS:
Shutoff valve, fixture shutoff valve, lavatory straight valve, cutoff valve, angle stop.

DESCRIPTION:
A small globe-type valve (page 187), usually chrome-plated, made of metal or plastic. Can be 90° (angle stop) or straight.

USE:
Controls water flow to the water supply tubes (page 158) connected to toilets, sinks, and other fixtures. Installed in accessible areas, such as inside sink cabinets and behind toilets, so they're easy to reach for repairs to the fixtures. Saves you from having to shut off water to the entire building.

USE TIPS:
The handle has great leverage, making it all too easy to strip the plastic kind. Take care.

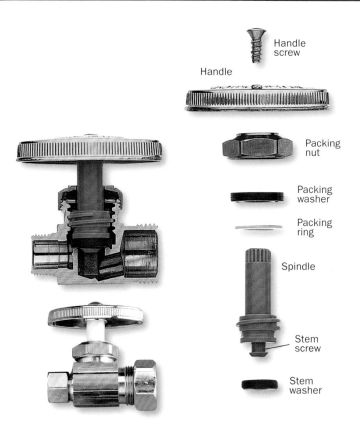

Water supply valve.

BUYING TIPS:

Using metal-stemmed valves limits the risk of stripping. If a valve leaks, you may be able to fix it by replacing the packing and/or stem washer, but usually this isn't worth the trouble—better to simply replace it. You have to shut off the building water in either case.

Ball Valve

DESCRIPTION:

Large lever controls an interior metal or plastic ball that covers or uncovers an opening for water.

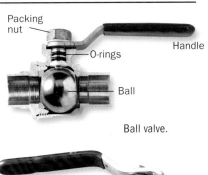

USE:

Controls water flow where quick action is a premium—one quick, easy twist of the lever and the valve is opened or closed. Commonly used for main shutoff valves on the incoming water supply to homes.

Ball valve.

BUYING TIPS:

Best valve available—shuts water off quickly and it's easy to see if valve is open or closed, unlike other valves.

Globe Valve

ALSO KNOWN AS:

Compression valve.

DESCRIPTION:

Rounded body with a seat on its bottom against which a stem with a replaceable washer presses. Rounded body is what gives this valve its name. Comes in most pipe sizes. Also available with openings at right angles to change the direction of the flow 90°, known as an *angle valve* (regular is called *straight*). A *connector globe valve* has a union fitting on one side, which, like the gate valve (page 188), is handy for connecting to radiators. Sillcocks (page 185) are usually globe valves.

Globe valve.

USE:

Controls water or steam flow, especially suitable for high pressure and frequent use.

USE TIPS:

Repair leaks around the handle by replacing the packing washer. If the valve does not stop water flow when closed, replace the stem washer.

Gate Valve

DESCRIPTION:

Faucet-like handle controlling a metal wedge that slides up and down into a seat. A *connector gate valve* has a union fitting on one side, handy when connecting to a radiator.

USE:

Controls water flow where total, unimpeded opening is required, such as on a water main, and is recommended wherever a constant flow is expected.

USE TIPS:

Usually best to keep completely, rather than partially, open or closed. Leaks from the stem often can be fixed (especially on radiators) by tightening the packing nut or else removing it and replacing the packing washer or, on older models, adding stem packing (page 178) underneath the nut.

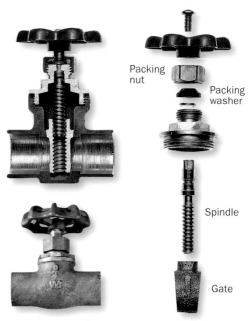

Packing nut

Packing washer

Spindle

Gate

Gate valve.

Drainable Valve

ALSO KNOWN AS:

Stop and waste valve, bleeder valve.

DESCRIPTION:

Essentially a globe or gate valve with a drain opening.

USE:

Draining pipe (on the non-pressure side) to prevent it from freezing in cold weather.

Saddle Valve

ALSO KNOWN AS:

Tap-on fitting.

DESCRIPTION:

Small water valve with a clamp assembly that fits over copper water supply piping. Once the clamp is installed and a water supply tube is connected to its outlet, the valve's handle is turned to drive a hollow needle (like an oversize hypodermic needle) into the wall of the copper pipe, completing the tap.

USE:

Quickly tapping into existing water supply pipe to hook up refrigerator ice makers and similar low-demand fixtures.

Saddle valve.

USE TIPS:

Do not confuse saddle valves with water supply valves (page 186); they are not shutoff valves. Use only in easily accessible (and visible) locations. Saddle valves are prone to leaking, and you want to spot trouble as soon as possible. Do not install them inside wall, floor, or ceiling cavities.

Check Valve

DESCRIPTION:

Regular and swing type, some for installation on vertical lines. Handleless valve with loose flap inside that closes when water flows the "wrong" way and swings open when it flows properly, allowing water to flow in one direction only.

USE:

To prevent backflow. Often used on vertical runs of piping that bring water from sump-pump basins to the outdoors.

USE TIP:

Models designed for use on vertical lines will not work if installed upside down; arrow on body denotes basic "open" direction.

CHAPTER 28

TOILET PARTS

ABOUT TOILETS

A toilet works in a surprisingly simple way, relying solely on water pressure and gravity to operate. When you push the handle, a lever pulls a chain that lifts a rubber flap (called a *flapper*) or a *tank ball* off the *flush valve*, a big hole in the center of the tank. Water from the tank rushes down through the valve and into the bowl. From there, the water takes a few turns through a *trap* inside the base of the bowl, creating suction that increases the force of the flush and sends the water and waste on their way to the sewer pipe.

While the basic process hasn't changed much, most of a toilet's parts have been refined and modified over the years. Today, new toilets use a fraction of the water that older models used, the old *ballcock*-style fill valve (the device that automatically refills the tank) and its coconut-shaped float have been replaced by a simpler plastic unit, and flappers have replaced tank balls. You can also retrofit an old toilet with a dual-flush device to dramatically reduce your household water use.

Standard toilet parts—fill valves, flappers, and levers—are inexpensive and easy to install, so repairing old mechanisms is largely a thing of the past. Toilet tanks are generally quite standard, and most have the same holes for the fill valve, flush valve, and tank bolts and handle. So even if you have an older toilet, chances are you can find new parts at any hardware store or home center.

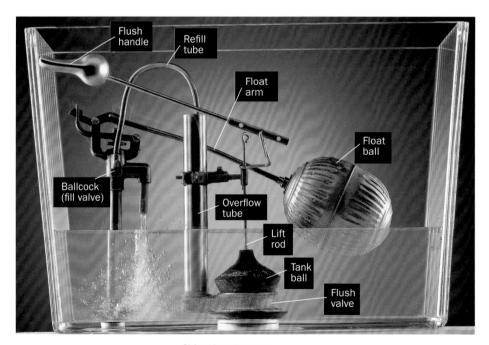

Old-style toilet parts.

Fill Valve

ALSO KNOWN AS:

Often mistakenly called a "ballcock" after the older version of this part.

DESCRIPTION:

Automatic valve mechanism with a plastic tower that mounts into a hole in the bottom of the toilet tank and connects to the water supply tube coming from the water supply valve below the toilet (see photo, page 186). One common brand, Fluidmaster®, has a cylindrical float that surrounds the tower and moves up and down with the water level, while another common brand, Korky®, has a stationary box near the top, called a float chamber, with a small float inside. Both have valves at the top that shut off the water supply when the desired water level is reached and small tubing that diverts some water into the overflow tube (page 194).

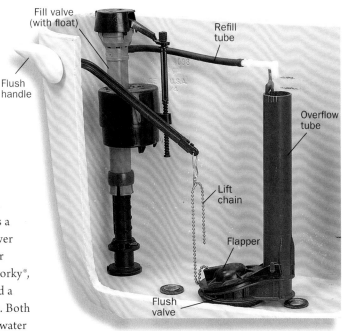

Contemporary toilet parts.

USE:

Controls water supply to refill the toilet tank. Activated by the change in water level. Standard modern replacement for traditional ballcock fill valves (page 192).

USE TIPS:

Follow directions carefully. Hand-tighten only, if possible, avoid using pliers, and do not overtighten—you might break the plastic or even the toilet tank. Carefully adjust so it works properly with desired water level. And don't forget to flush after turning off the water supply (*Reminder: Turn off the water first!*). Have a sponge and bucket or kitchen storage box ready for collecting the water from the tank.

BUYING TIPS:

Inexpensive and relatively easy to install, especially if your toilet supply line and tank are easily accessible. If you have more than a couple of toilets in your house, keep a spare around. Be warned: some toilet manufacturers use proprietary fill valves that do not have generic replacements.

Ballcock Repair Kit

DESCRIPTION:

Repair for older ballcock fill valves, which typically have a diaphragm-type valve on top. Repair kits may contain replacement caps for the valve and replacement diaphragms (upper and lower).

USE:

Repairing ballcocks that leak into the tank and/or don't fill properly.

BUYING TIPS:

You can still find these repair kits for ballcocks, as well as replacement float arms and float balls, but the fact is, a repair kit alone can cost as much as an entire new-style fill valve (typically under $10), which has its own float and no need for a float arm.

Flapper

ALSO KNOWN AS:

Flapper valve.

DESCRIPTION:

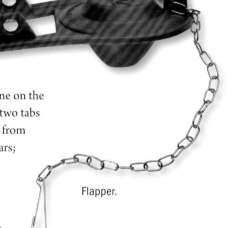

The trapdoor-like device that opens and closes over the flush valve in the bottom of the toilet tank. Standard version has a roughly round rubber flap with a raised center portion on the top and a protruding cone on the bottom. Ears extend from the back of the flap; these hook onto two tabs on the overflow tube or flush valve assembly. A chain extending from the toilet handle hooks onto the edge of the flap, opposite the ears; this lifts the flapper to initiate the flush.

Flapper.

USE:

Controls water flow from bottom of tank. When it is lifted the tank water rushes out and flushing is started. Flappers are easy and effective replacements for old-style tank balls, which are prone to leaking over time.

BUYING TIPS:

"Universal" flappers are designed to fit most standard toilets, new and old. If you can't find a good fit, bring the old flapper or tank ball to a well-stocked store or plumbing supply house for identification.

Toilet Flush Handle

ALSO KNOWN AS:
Toilet flush lever, toilet tank lever, toilet trip lever.

DESCRIPTION:
Lever on front (or side) of tank. Usually supplied with the lever or arm attached. Available in plastic, chromed plastic, and various metals, including brass, bronze, nickel, and stainless steel.

USE:
Raises flapper (or tank ball, on older toilets) to initiate flush.

USE TIPS:
Unlike most things, to remove the handle, unscrew in a clockwise direction. It is held on by a *left-hand–threaded* nut. Be careful not to overtighten the nut and risk cracking the tank.

Flush Valve & Repair Kit

ALSO KNOWN AS:
Flush valve seat, flush ball seat, tank outlet, seat.

DESCRIPTION:
Flush valve is a large, round fitting at the bottom of the toilet tank, made of metal or plastic. Typically includes the *overflow tube* extending vertically from the valve. Valve assembly is secured with a large *spud nut* on the underside of the tank. Replacing the valve requires removing the tank and using a special wrench called a spud wrench or very large tongue-and-groove pliers. A *flush valve repair kit* contains a new plastic ring that fits inside the old flush valve so you don't have to replace it. Ring is adhered to valve with self-adhesive backing or silicone caulk. Kit includes a new flapper sized for the repair ring.

USE:
Replacing or repairing old flush valves, which can corrode or develop mineral buildup over time and fail to seal properly with the flapper, leaking water into the bowl.

BUYING TIPS:
Repairing a valve is much easier than replacing one. The kits typically cost less than $10, so it's at least worth a try.

Refill Tube

ALSO KNOWN AS:
Bowl refill tube.

DESCRIPTION:
Small tube that slips over a nipple on the fill valve and connects to a clip on the top edge of the overflow tube. Contemporary versions typically made of vinyl; older models may be brass or aluminum.

USE:
Fills bowl with water after flushing to keep sewer odors out.

BUYING TIPS:
If you're replacing a fill valve (page 191), the new unit will include a refill tube, but you can buy tubes separately. New tube typically includes a new plastic or metal clip for connecting to the overflow tube.

Overflow Tube

DESCRIPTION:
Plastic, copper, brass, or aluminum tube 1 or 1⅛ inches in diameter that screws into flush valve (page 193).

BUYING TIPS:
Packaged with *flush valves* or individually. Get the largest thickness (gauge) available, and avoid aluminum, which corrodes quickly.

Tank-to-Bowl Attachment Hardware

ALSO KNOWN AS:
Tank bolts, spud washer.

Tank bolts (with washers and nuts) and spud washer.

DESCRIPTION:
Long brass bolts with large rubber washers and a bagel-sized, foam-rubber washer, sometimes called a *spud washer*. These items are usually available in small packages. Standard size for all brands.

USE:
Anchoring the tank to the bowl on a standard two-piece toilet. The two brass bolts and washers go in small holes at the bottom of the tank and through holes in the platform

at the back of the bowl, and are secured under the platform with nuts. The spud washer fits around the bottom end of the flush valve (page 193) to create a seal between the tank and bowl.

Closet Flange Bolt

Closet bolts.

ALSO KNOWN AS:
Closet bolt, toilet bolt, hold-down bolt.

DESCRIPTION:
Long brass bolts with large heads that have two flat sides to keep the bolts from turning. The bolts are inserted heads-down into keyhole slots in the *closet flange*, the large, round, plastic fitting mounted to the floor at the top end of the toilet's drain pipe. The closet bolts extend up through the hole at each side of the toilet bowl base and are secured with washers and nuts. A variation is the *closet screw*, which has wood-screw threads on one end for anchoring the toilet base to a wooden floor.

USE:
Secures toilet base to closet flange or floor.

Wax Ring

Wax ring.

DESCRIPTION:
Thick wax ring, typically with a plastic flange that extends down through the bottom of the ring. Designed to fit standard 3- and 4-inch toilet drain openings.

USE:
Creates a watertight seal between the base of the toilet bowl and the closet flange at the top end of the toilet's drain pipe. Used when installing new toilets or when an existing toilet has been removed for any reason.

USE TIPS:
Wax rings are not reusable and must be replaced any time the toilet base has been lifted up or repositioned. When installing a new ring you get only one chance to position the toilet; if you have to remove the toilet base after the wax ring is compressed, replace the ring.

BUYING TIPS:
Available in standard and double-height versions. There are also "no-wax" toilet seals sold as an alternative to traditional wax rings. Manufacturers claim no-mess convenience and a more universal fit when compared to conventional rings.

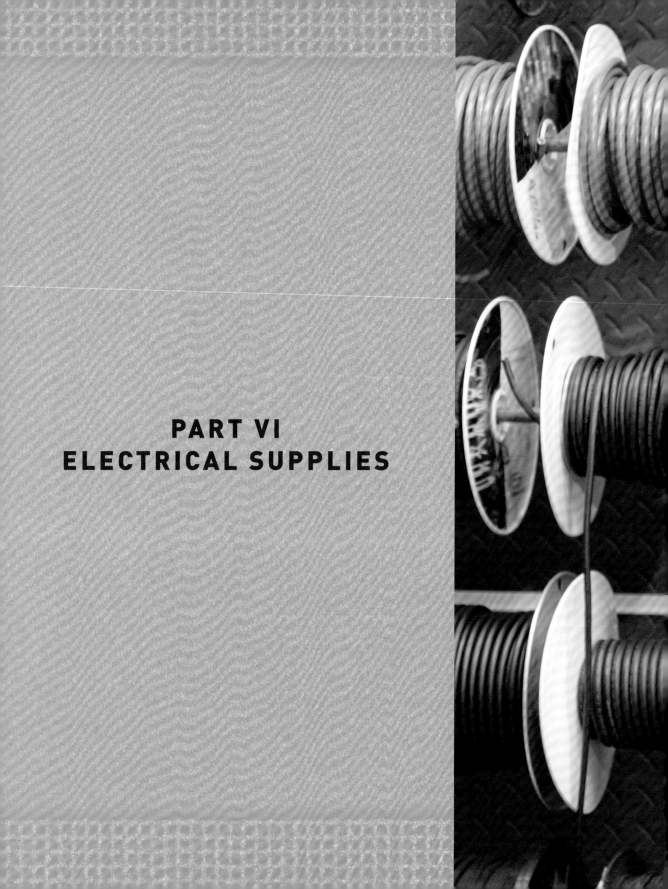

PART VI
ELECTRICAL SUPPLIES

ABOUT ELECTRICAL & BUILDING CODES

The type of electrical product used and the way it is installed are governed by local building codes throughout the country. Most local codes are based on the National Electrical Code book (commonly known as the NEC), which is published by the National Fire Protection Association and updated every three years. Codes are enforceable laws that must be checked out before you make any major installations. Many codes prohibit the use of some of the items listed here, even though they are mostly standard equipment. See page 148 (intro to plumbing chapter) for more information on codes and permits.

ABOUT HOUSEHOLD WIRING

Standard household wiring is rated for 120 volts, although this may be referred to as 110, 115, or 125 volts—which for most replacement purposes means the same thing. Standard circuits—those used for lighting and regular receptacles (outlets) in living areas—are rated for 15 amps of current. Therefore, the most standard circuit is a 120-volt, 15-amp circuit. Receptacles in kitchens, garages, bathrooms, and utility areas are commonly rated for 120 volts and 20 amps to provide a little more power for the relatively high demands of appliances and tools. Circuits for high-voltage appliances, such as electric clothes dryers, ranges, and baseboard heaters, operate on 240 volts (also called 220, 230, or 250; again, same thing) and amperages of 20 to 50 amps.

You need to understand these circuit basics when selecting switches, receptacles, wiring, and other devices, because all electrical equipment is rated for specific circuit voltage and amperage. Always use wiring and devices with the same ratings as the circuit they will be installed on. For example, use a 120-volt, 15-amp switch for a standard 15-amp circuit, and use a 120-volt, 20-amp receptacle only on a standard 20-amp circuit.

You also need to know the type of wiring you have. If your house was built before the 1960s or after the 1970s, chances are it has wiring made of solid copper, which is still the standard for new construction and remodeling. Devices for use with solid copper are labeled "COPPER" or "CU."

Some houses built in the 1960s and 1970s have solid aluminum or copper-coated (copper-clad) aluminum wiring. Aluminum wiring has been linked to numerous house fires and other electrical hazards, due to its high rate of expansion and contraction and to the presence of corrosion when it's connected to electrical devices made for copper wiring. Both of these problems can cause the wiring to come loose from their connections. Aluminum wiring can be safe if it is connected to the proper type of devices. Devices labeled "CO/ALR" are intended for use with solid aluminum wiring. Those labeled "CU-CLAD ONLY" are intended for copper-coated aluminum. In any case, it's a good idea to consult an electrician if you have aluminum wiring.

ABOUT POLARIZED PLUGS & GROUNDING

Polarized plugs have one wide blade (or prong) and one narrow blade and must be oriented correctly to fit into the wide and narrow slots in almost all receptacles. They've been around for about a century, although most of us consider them a "modern" annoyance. Polarization is a safety feature that prevents the "hot" wiring from crossing with the neutral wiring. The third blade, or prong—on a plug that has one— is the ground prong. It provides a path for electricity to follow if something goes wrong, such as a wire coming loose and touching the metal side of an electrical box, creating a short circuit, or fault.

All standard modern receptacles are polarized and include a grounding slot. Many, but not all, plugs include a ground prong. Appliances and devices with plugs that don't have ground prongs are internally insulated and/or have insulating housings to protect you from a shock if there's a short inside the appliance.

Grounding is a safety system that connects each electrical device in a house to the main service panel (breaker box) and in turn to a ground rod (or other means) buried in the earth. In most cases, devices are grounded through the green-insulated or bare-copper ground wire in the circuit cable(s) connecting the device. Just because a receptacle has a ground slot doesn't mean it's properly grounded. If you're replacing a receptacle, switch, light fixture, etc. and discover there is no ground wire in the circuit cable(s) inside the electrical box, that's something you'll have to address. The device will probably work fine without a ground, but it won't be as safe or be up to code.

Two-slot/two-prong polarized receptacle and plug.

Grounding prong

Three-slot/three-prong grounded receptacle and plug.

CHAPTER 29

EXTENSION CORDS, PLUGS & POWER STRIPS

Extension Cords

DESCRIPTION:

Available in various lengths from 3 to 100 feet and in various colors; wire may be two-wire or the heavier three-wire grounded type (recommended). Extension cords are typically supplied with a female plug on one end and a male plug on the other. Latest innovations are a cord with three female receptacles and another with a receptacle box with six female receptacles and a built-in *circuit breaker* or ground-fault circuit-interrupter (GFCI) device (page 218), sometimes called a *portable outlet center*.

USE:

Provides power at a remote location.

USE TIPS:

Extension cords are sized to handle a certain amount of current and should be matched to the device(s) they are powering. For example, household-type extension cords are suitable for lamps, fans, small electronics, and other low-demand devices. High-amperage appliances, such as portable heaters, can overheat lightweight cords and create a fire hazard. Heavy-duty, grounded cords are suitable for power tools and other high-amperage devices. Check the amperage (amp) rating on the cord; this should be higher than the amp draw of all devices it is powering. Use only GFCI-protected cords for outdoor work.

BUYING TIPS:

Flat plug extension cords are ideal for plugging in behind furniture because the plug and cord install flush to the outlet and wall. Some types have swiveling plugs for positioning the cord wherever you want it.

Standard Plug

ALSO KNOWN AS:

Replacement plug, electrical plug, grounding plug.

DESCRIPTION:

Male plug with two or three prongs. Plugs may be of light or heavy construction, such as black rubber (for appliances) or light plastic in brown, black, and/or ivory. *Side-outlet* plugs have the wire coming out the side. Plugs for very light-duty cords may simply snap onto cords, making electrical contact with metal teeth that bite through the cord insulation. Better, heavier-duty plugs have screw terminals for connecting the bare-wire ends of the cord wires. Screw terminals are preferable in any case.

USE:

Replacing an old or damaged plug on an extension cord or appliance power cord.

USE TIPS:

Make sure the plug is the right type and suitably rated for the cord it will be installed on. For example, use only grounded plugs for a grounded (three-wire) extension cord. The amperage rating of the plug must meet or exceed the rating of the cord or appliance. Do not replace the plug on a high-voltage appliance cord, such as for a clothes dryer, electric range, or air conditioner; instead, replace the entire cord with an appliance power cord (below).

Replacement plug (disassembled).

Appliance Cord

ALSO KNOWN AS:

Appliance power cord, dryer pigtail, range pigtail.

DESCRIPTION:

Insulated cord with male plug on one end and female plug or individual wire connectors on the other end. Each cord is for use with a specific appliance, such as a clothes dryer, electric range or cooktop, or air conditioner.

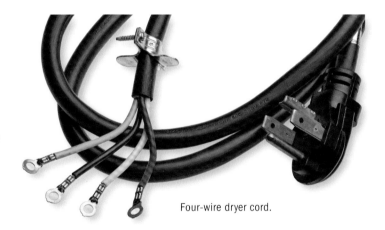

Four-wire dryer cord.

USE:

New or replacement power cord for a specific electrical appliance. New dryers and ranges typically are sold without power cords, which must be purchased separately.

USE TIPS:

Warning: Do not plug in an appliance cord before it is fully connected to the appliance! Dryer and range cords typically have loose wire ends that are live when the plug is inserted into the wall outlet. When live, the ends can deliver deadly current if they touch you and will result in a short circuit if they touch each other.

BUYING TIPS:

Dryer and range cords are similar but are not interchangeable; use the right type for your appliance. Dryer cords come in three-wire and four-wire versions; the former are found on older appliances and fit three-slot dryer outlets, while four-wire are the new standard and are required by most codes for new appliances and installations. Make sure the cord carries the proper amperage and voltage ratings for your appliance. When in doubt, have an electrician or appliance technician install your cord.

3-to-2 Adapter Plug

ALSO KNOWN AS:
Grounding adapter, plug adapter, cheater plug.

DESCRIPTION:
Small, cube-shaped plastic or rubber plug with two prongs on one end and three openings in the other, with a small, U-shaped metal piece (lug) attached directly to the plug. Older models may have a 3-inch grounding wire (lead)—usually green in color—coming directly out of the middle, with the U-shaped lug on its end.

3-to-2 adapter plug.

USE:
Allows use of three-pronged (grounded) plug in a two-slot receptacle.

USE TIPS:
Note that while the adapter does the job of getting power to the cord, it seldom actually grounds the plug and cord, for several reasons. First, two-prong receptacles often are not grounded to begin with; using a "grounding plug" offers no grounding protection whatsoever. Second, for the ground lug to be effective it must be connected to the central screw on the receptacle, the one that secures the coverplate; most users fail to do this. Using the ground lug works only if the electrical box is metal (can't be plastic, as most modern boxes are) *and* it is grounded through a means called *bonding*, which often is unreliable. Finally, even if the box is grounded this is a weak ground connection at best and therefore a poor method of grounding protection. Bottom line: use at your own risk.

Power Strip

DESCRIPTION:
Rectangular plastic strip containing multiple receptacles and a cord to plug into a nearby outlet. Available in a wide range of sizes and styles, some featuring just a few receptacles, others, more than a dozen. Cord length also varies, up to about 8 feet. Some models have built-in circuit breakers for overload protection, but this does not make the strip a surge protector (page 203). Many of today's power strips include USB ports for charging computers and other electronics. Some have home automation (smart home) functions, such as timer control and remote operation through a phone.

USE:

Multiplies the capacity of a single outlet at a convenient location. Helps manage multiple power cords neatly.

USE TIP:

Power strips with ON/OFF buttons allow you to control all devices plugged into the strip. This helps save energy with things such as phone and computer chargers and electronics with "standby" mode or power lights, all of which consume electricity even when they're sitting unused.

Surge Protector

ALSO KNOWN AS:

Surge suppressor.

DESCRIPTION:

Models for home use are essentially power strips (page 202) with internal devices for surge protection. This means they help absorb spikes or surges in the electrical system caused by a nearby lighting strike or when the power comes back on after being shut down (as well as numerous other causes).

Surge protector.

USE:

Powering and protecting sensitive—and expensive—electronic equipment, such as computers, TVs, audio/video equipment, etc.

NOTE:

A surge protector must be plugged into a properly grounded outlet to offer surge protection; it's best if the outlet has a true ground provided by a ground wire in the circuit cable. A GFCI outlet (page 218) that is not grounded offers ground-fault protection, but it is not a true ground and will not support surge protection.

BUYING TIPS:

Don't assume a power strip offer surge protection just because it has a breaker or an ON/OFF switch. Surge suppression capability is rated in *joules*. For example, a surge protector rated for 1,000 joules can absorb surges totaling 1,000 joules. This may be in the form of 10 surges of 100 joules each or 1 surge of 1,000 joules, or another combination. The surge protection effectively gets used up, so after it hits the 1,000-joules mark it no longer offers surge protection and should be replaced. How many joules you need depends on the equipment you're protecting and the likelihood of surges in your home.

Multiple-Outlet Taps & Adapters

ALSO KNOWN AS:
Multi-outlet, plug-in strip, plug-in outlet adapter, outlet tap, table tap, cube tap.

DESCRIPTION:
One-piece plastic units in various sizes, shapes, and configurations, containing two to six sets of slots for plugs. Comes either with third grounding prong or not. Some multi-outlet adapters have a long machine screw for screwing into a duplex wall receptacle (replacing the outlet coverplate) for semi-permanent installation.

USE:
Plugs into any outlet to provide multiple receptacle capacity.

BUYING TIPS:
Choose only grounded taps and adapters, which work with three-prong (grounded) and two-prong (polarized) plugs.

Five-outlet adapter.

ABOUT SOCKET ADAPTERS

Socket adapters, sometimes called *current taps*, differ from the taps and adapters described above, in that they screw into sockets rather than plug into outlets. They also should be used sparingly and are generally intended for temporary use, although if used appropriately, they work as well as permanent products. However, these devices—and anything plugged into them—are not grounded.

Lamp-holder is the industry term for a socket, the device that holds a light bulb (called a *lamp* in the industry), as well as for the basic porcelain or plastic light fixture that holds a single light bulb (see page 206).

Socket Adapter

TYPES:

Socket-to-lamp-holder/outlet adapter
Lamp-holder-to-outlet adapter
Single-to-twin lamp-holder adapter

DESCRIPTION & USE:

SOCKET-TO-LAMP-HOLDER/OUTLET ADAPTER:

Round plastic device with light- bulb–like threads on each end (male on one, female on the other) and receptacle slots on each side. Some models have a pull chain or toggle switch that turns off the bulb but not the outlets. If it has no pull chain, it is called a *keyless adapter*. Provides two outlets wherever there's a light socket, without sacrificing the bulb.

PLUG TO LAMP-HOLDER ADAPTER:

Two-prong plug on one end, lamp-holder socket on the other.

SINGLE-TO-TWIN LAMP-HOLDER ADAPTER:

Also called a *twin light adapter*. V-shaped device that holds two light bulbs at an angle to each other, with one threaded end that screws into a regular socket. Provides a double socket in the place of a single.

USE TIPS:

Do not exceed the maximum wattage rating of the socket/light fixture with anything plugged into the adapter. Use LED light bulbs in the sockets to minimize the wattage used up by the lights.

Plug to lamp-
holder adapter.

Socket-to-lamp-
holder/outlet adapter.

Single-to-twin
lamp-holder adapter.

CHAPTER 30

LAMP & LIGHT FIXTURE REPAIR PARTS

Light Socket

ALSO KNOWN AS:
Incandescent lamp holder, light bulb socket.

DESCRIPTION:
Cylindrical assembly consisting of a removable metal *shell* surrounding a threaded metal *socket* (where the light bulb screws in), and a plastic base that houses the switch (as applicable) and two screw terminals for the wiring connections. Some sockets don't have a switch, because the fixture has a separate switch or is controlled by a wall switch. Some sockets have two wire leads extending from the socket base, rather than screw terminals. Sockets with terminals typically have one brass and one silver screw, for each electrical supply wire.

Light socket with screw terminals and switch.

Light socket with wire leads (no switch).

USE:
Replacement socket for light fixtures of all descriptions. Light-bulb bases—and therefore socket sizes—have remained standard for many years; it's easy to find a socket for almost any fixture, even if the part doesn't exactly match the original.

USE TIPS:
Secure cord wires inside a socket with an Underwriter's knot, whenever possible. Fixture and lamp cord is polarized: The wire with the ribbed or marked insulation is the neutral wire and connects to the silver screw terminal or white wire lead on the socket; the other wire is "hot" and connects to the brass terminal or black lead. Standard sockets are compatible with traditional incandescent light bulbs as well as energy-efficient (LED and compact fluorescent) bulbs.

ABOUT LAMP PARTS

Lamps are almost infinitely repairable, regardless of their age or type. If you take apart a lamp (unplugged, of course), you'll discover that the base is merely a hollow structure that holds a few simple electrical parts. Replacing any or all of those parts will get your old lamp working like new while looking like it always has. If you aren't crazy with how it's always looked, you can replace the shade—something you're more likely to find at a lighting store than a hardware supplier.

Lamp parts.

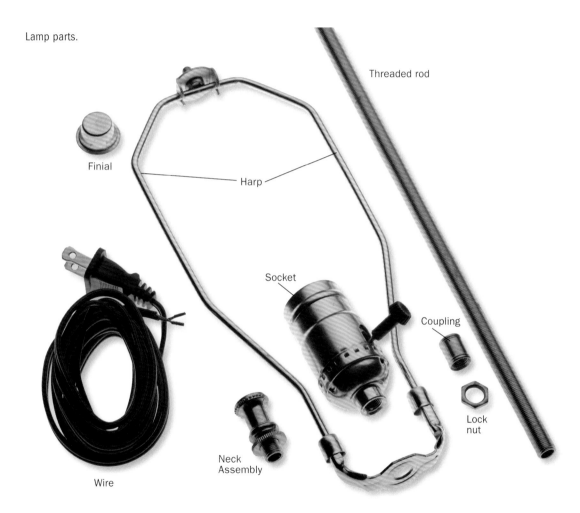

Finial

Threaded rod

Harp

Socket

Coupling

Lock nut

Neck Assembly

Wire

Lamp Parts

PART:

Finial

Harp

Clip adapter

Socket

Threaded rod (also known as *all-thread*)

Coupling

Locknut

Reducing bushing

Wire (also known as *lamp cord* and *flexible cord*)

DESCRIPTION & USE:

FINIAL:

Small, decorative cap with female threads in one end. Screws on to secure lampshade to top of *harp*.

HARP:

Oblong-shaped wire frame with a connecting fitting at its bottom end. Holds the lampshade.

CLIP ADAPTER:

Two oblong wire forms with stems in a metal piece that has a short threaded rod. Clips onto bulb and is used when a lamp has no harp to hold the lampshade.

SOCKET:

Cylindrical part where the light bulb is screwed in. May or may not contain a switch. Lamp sockets are the same as other standard light fixture sockets.

THREADED ROD:

Hollow metal tube threaded on the outside along its entire length. Standard lamp rod has an outside diameter of $3/8$ inch. Serves as the spine of the lamp. The lamp wire runs through it and many of the lamp parts are supported by it.

COUPLING:

Small, tube-like fitting threaded on the inside. Used for joining two lengths of threaded rod.

LOCKNUT:

Small, flat metal ring, sometimes with an opening and a slight spiral shape, sometimes hexagonal. Secures various parts to the threaded rod.

REDUCING BUSHING:

Small, round fitting threaded on the inside and outside. Reduces the inside diameter of rod from ¼ to ⅛ inch to change from one rod size to another.

WIRE:

Lamp wire type is 18-2 SPT-1 and may be bought with or without a plug. Provides electrical power. Typically, the same cord runs from the plug and up through the lamp base and threaded rod and any extending arms (hollow, like the rod) and connects to the socket. If a lamp has multiple sockets, the cord wires may be connected to multiple wire leads inside the lamp base.

BUYING TIPS:

Lamp parts are sold in kits and as individual parts. Kits are often better for building new lamps or completely refurbishing old lamps, while individual parts can be more economical for repairs. Sockets may also be bought individually and can result in slight savings for repairs. *Socket reducers* that screw into a standard-size socket (called *Edison*, or *E26*, base) and permit use of bulbs with small candelabra bases are available.

Fluorescent Light Fixture Parts

DESCRIPTION:

Replacement parts for utility-type fluorescent fixtures—the kind that take the long tube lamps (bulbs)— include the *starter* (a small metal cylinder typically found on each side of the fixture housing on older fixtures); *sockets* (the tombstone-shaped fittings that receive the pins of the fluorescent lamps); and the *ballast* (a black metal box usually housed inside the fixture, behind a coverplate that also conceals the fixture wiring). The ballast lowers the incoming voltage for use in the fixture. Newer, rapid-start fixtures have a starter and ballast in one piece.

USE:

Replacing worn parts on fluorescent light fixtures.

USE TIPS:

If a lamp flickers and won't go on all the way, or it won't go on at all, the problem may be the lamp itself, the starter, or the ballast. Start by testing with a good lamp. Failing that, replace the starter (very inexpensive).

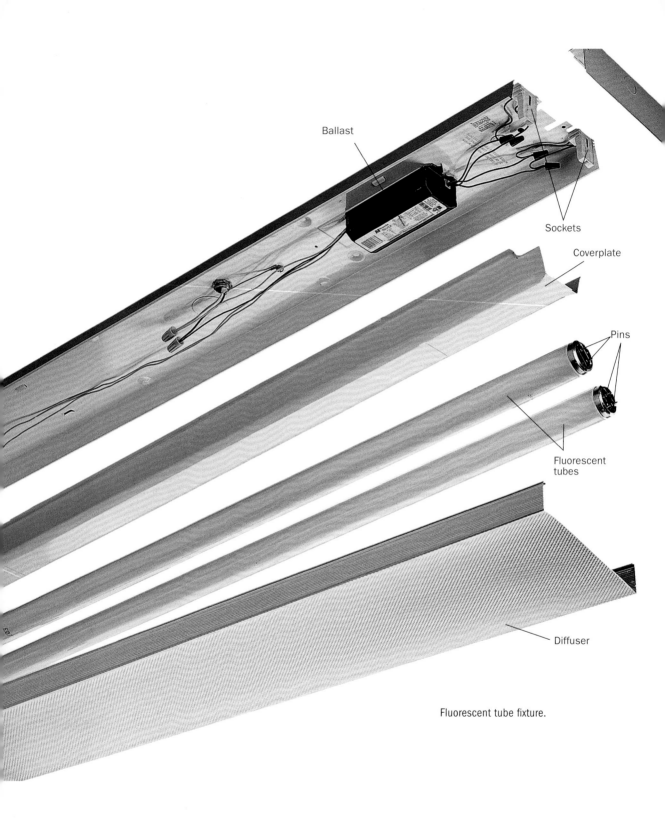

Ballast

Sockets

Coverplate

Pins

Fluorescent
tubes

Diffuser

Fluorescent tube fixture.

If that doesn't help, you may need to replace the ballast, but check the pricing on the part—often it makes more sense to replace the entire fixture. Ballasts that hum loudly or are leaking an oily black substance also need replacement. Replace a socket that is scorched, cracked, loose, or otherwise damaged—also an inexpensive fix. New parts must match those being replaced.

Starter.

CHAPTER 31

SWITCHES & RECEPTACLES

ABOUT SWITCHES

Switches function by interrupting electrical flow. There are many types of switches, but most can be categorized as either those linked to the main house wiring or those that are used elsewhere, such as on cords of light fixtures and other electrical devices. When replacing switches, find a suitable match by looking at the number of terminals, the wiring type, and the amperage and voltage ratings.

Standard Light Switches

TYPES:

Single-pole switch

Three-way switch

Four-way switch

DESCRIPTION & USE:

Ordinary wall-mounted switches for light fixtures, vent fans, ceiling fans, etc. May have a toggle lever or rocker-style control or special features such as illuminated toggle or rocker or night-light display. Typically 120 volts and either 15 or 20 amp. The difference in appearance and application among the three main types is evident in the number of screw terminals (where the wires are attached):

SINGLE-POLE:

Simplest switch style, with two brass screw terminals plus a ground screw. Those with toggle levers typically have ON/OFF markings. Used to control one or more fixtures from a single location.

THREE-WAY:

Contains two brass (typically) *traveler* terminals and one darker-colored *common* screw terminal, plus a ground screw. Toggle lever has no ON/OFF markings. Used for controlling one or more fixtures from two different locations, such as at the top and bottom of a staircase.

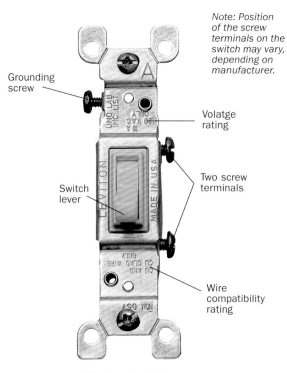

Note: Position of the screw terminals on the switch may vary, depending on manufacturer.

Grounding screw

Volatge rating

Switch lever

Two screw terminals

Wire compatibility rating

Single-pole switch.

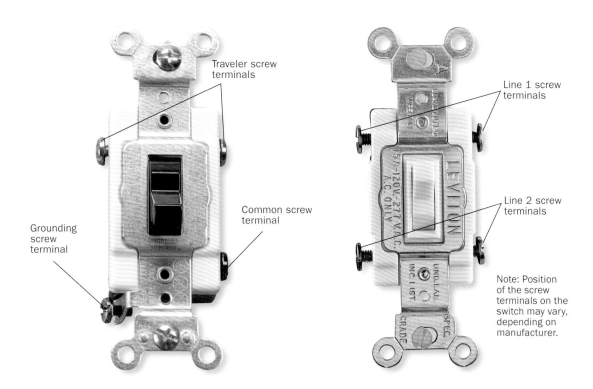

Three-way switch.

Four-way switch.

Traveler screw terminals

Grounding screw terminal

Common screw terminal

Line 1 screw terminals

Line 2 screw terminals

Note: Position of the screw terminals on the switch may vary, depending on manufacturer.

FOUR-WAY:

Contains two *Line 1* screw terminals and two *Line 2* terminals, plus a ground screw. Toggle lever has no ON/OFF markings. Always installed between a pair of three-way switches, enabling control of fixtures from three locations.

USE TIPS:

Use screw terminals or push-in fittings (on the back side of switch) that include a screw for clamping down on each wire after it's pushed in. Avoid using push-in fittings without clamps, which may not hold wiring securely.

BUYING TIPS:

It's often worth it to pay an extra dollar or two to upgrade to a "preferred" or "premium" switch. The cheapest options feel flimsy and probably won't last as long as the better models.

Dimmer Switch

ALSO KNOWN AS:

Rheostat.

DESCRIPTION:

Light switch with a boxy housing and (typically) three or more wire leads for connecting to household circuit wiring. Dimmer controls come in a variety of types and styles, such as dial, slider, rocker, and toggle. Some have a regular ON/OFF control switch and a small slider control on the side for setting the dimmer level. Most dimmers are single-pole switches (see page 212), but three-way versions are available.

USE:

Adjusting light levels on permanently installed light fixtures (not lamps and other portable devices).

USE TIPS:

Dimmer switch bodies produce some heat that must be dissipated. Do not crowd them in a small switch box or a box filled with wiring.

Slider-type dimmer switch.

BUYING TIPS:

Not all dimmers are compatible or fully functional with energy-efficient LED and CFL light bulbs. Nor are all LEDs and, especially, CFL bulbs, dimmable. For the best performance, choose a dimmer designed for the light bulb you will use. Most LEDs will work with conventional dimmers but may not offer full light adjustability (they may shut off a little early and start up a little late at the low end of the dimmer range, for example). CFLs often must be an expensive dimmable type to work with conventional dimmers.

Specialty Switches

TYPES:

Double switch
Combination switch/receptacle
Pilot light switch
Timer switch
Motion-sensor switch

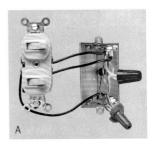

DESCRIPTION & USE:

A. DOUBLE SWITCH:

Light switch with two switch controls, typically either toggle or rocker-style. Used to control two different fixtures from a single location.

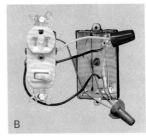

B. COMBINATION SWITCH/RECEPTACLE:

Single unit with a small toggle or rocker switch and a standard grounded (three-slot) receptacle. Used where receptacles are scarce or where you want to control a plugged-in device using a wall switch. Can be wired so the receptacle turns on and off with the switch or has power at all times.

C. PILOT LIGHT SWITCH:

Switch with a small light on its face that is illuminated at all times. Used in basements, garages, and similar areas to help you locate the switch in the dark.

D. TIMER SWITCH:

Includes timer control that turns fixture on/off at a preset interval. Available in a variety of types, including *countdown* (often used for bathroom vent fans; shuts off fan after a preset time), *programmable* (security lights, heating appliances), *spring-wound* (works like an old-fashioned kitchen timer), *occupancy-sensor* (turns on if it senses movement; turns off automatically), and *daylight-sensor* (turns on when ambient light gets low, or at sunset).

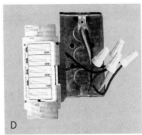

E. OCCUPANCY-SENSOR SWITCH:

Also called *motion-sensor* or *motion-detector* switch. Light switch that turns on automatically when you enter the room and will turn off after a preset period if the room is vacant or if there is no movement. Often used in public buildings, where people tend to leave the lights on; in garages and basements for convenience; and for security lighting.

Line Switch

ALSO KNOWN AS:

In-line switch, feed-through switch, lamp cord switch.

DESCRIPTION:

Light-duty switch that installs onto an electrical cord. Standard type has a body consisting of two, separable plastic halves that have prongs inside that push through the wire's insulation when the halves are screwed back together, making electrical contact. Most have a knurled wheel or a toggle for the switch control. Better versions often have larger plastic bodies and toggles.

Line switch.

USE:

On/off control of lamps and similar light-duty fixtures.

USE TIPS:

Line switches are suitable for lamps and other light-duty, plug-in fixtures and appliances. They should not be used on extension cords or any system that exceeds their voltage and amperage ratings. Standard lamp-cord versions are sized for 18-gauge lamp cord (page 222). Do not use a switch that does not fit properly over the cord; if the cord insulation is too thick, use a larger switch.

Canopy Switch

DESCRIPTION:

Small switch with quarter-sized, typically round, plastic body with rotary, toggle, push-button, or pull-chain switch extending from its center. Includes wire leads for connecting to fixture wiring. Often with a threaded post (surrounding switch lever or button) and nut for mounting switch into lamp bases or fixture housings. Versions for ceiling fans typically offer three-speed control.

USE:

On/off and speed control of lamps, ceiling fans, and similar light-duty fixtures.

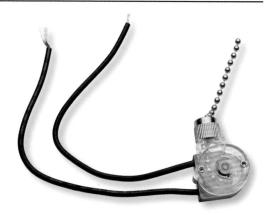

Canopy switch.

ABOUT RECEPTACLES

Receptacles, commonly called outlets, come in a few different types. Whether you're replacing old receptacles or adding receptacles to new circuits, it's important to know which type is required for the application. Local code may specify AFCI receptacles (page 219) for most living areas, including hallways and kitchens, while GFCI receptacles (page 218) are almost certainly required for locations along kitchen countertops and in bathrooms, garages, and areas near sinks, as well as outdoors.

Standard Receptacle

ALSO KNOWN AS:

Outlet (technically incorrect).

DESCRIPTION:

Standard *duplex* receptacle has two sets of slots for grounded (three-prong) plugs. They have four screw terminals—two silver terminals for neutral wires and two brass terminals for "hot" wires—plus a ground screw. They also have metal connecting tabs between the terminals on each side; these can be removed for specific wiring configurations, such as wiring each half of the receptacle to its own circuit. (Technically, an "outlet" is just the point at which current is supplied, i.e., where the receptacle is installed.)

In addition to their stamped ratings, standard receptacles are identifiable by their appearance:

15-amp duplex receptacle.

20-amp duplex receptacle.

15-AMP

receptacles have two vertical slots and a ground slot in each plug set.

20-AMP

receptacles have a sideways T-shaped slot on the left and a vertical slot on the right, plus a ground slot. The special T-slot is compatible with 20-amp plugs, which have two straight blades perpendicular to each other (plus a ground prong).

USE:

Provides an electrical connection for power cords with plugs.

USE TIPS:

Like switches, receptacles may have push-in fittings on the backs of the devices, in addition to screw terminals. Better models have screws that clamp down on the wires after they're pushed in. Many experts recommend using only screw terminals or push-in fittings with clamping screw clamps—especially for receptacles, which suffer a lot of abuse from plugs going in and out. Push-in fittings without clamping screws are more prone to coming loose over time.

BUYING TIPS:

Also like switches, it's worth it to pay a little more for an upgraded receptacle. The cheapest options won't last as long and are more likely to lose their grip on plugs over time.

Appliance Receptacle

DESCRIPTION USE:

Single-plug receptacle with three or four slots in various shapes and configurations for use with specific appliance plugs. Three types of appliance receptacles are common in households:

20-AMP, 240-VOLT:

One T-slot, one horizontal straight slot, and a ground slot. Typically used for room/portable air conditioners.

30-AMP, 120/240-VOLT:

Two straight slots, one L-shaped slot, and a ground slot. Used for electric clothes dryers. Provides 240-volt current for the dryer's heating element and 120-volt current for timers, lights, electronics, etc.

50-AMP, 120/240-VOLT:

Three straight slots and a ground slot. Used for electric ranges. Provides 240-volt current for heating elements and 120-volt current for electronics, lights, etc.

Ground-Fault Circuit-Interrupter (GFCI) Receptacle

ALSO KNOWN AS:

GFI (incorrect).

DESCRIPTION:

GFCI receptacle is a standard-voltage (120 volts) duplex receptacle with a flat face and two buttons on the front. It contains a sensor device and a circuit breaker that trips if the device senses a change in the electrical current (caused by a ground fault), shutting off the power to the receptacle. A ground fault might be caused by a tool or appliance with a loose wire or when electricity contacts water, such as when someone drops a hair dryer in the bathtub (extreme example). Pressing the TEST button on the front of the receptacle trips the breaker manually. Pressing the RESET button resets the breaker after a manual test or when the breaker trips on its own. Fancy circuitry aside, a GFCI receptacle works just like any other household receptacle.

GFCI receptacle
(20-amp version shown).

USE:

The GFCI's job is to sense hazardous leakage of electricity instantaneously and shut off the circuit. It works far faster than a standard circuit breaker or fuse. A GFCI receptacle can be wired to offer its circuit-sensing protection at one receptacle only, or it can be wired to protect itself and every receptacle beyond it on the same circuit. In addition to GFCI receptacles, there are GFCI circuit breakers, which provide the same protection to all devices on a circuit. There are also GFCI extension cords for use outdoors or in wet areas.

USE TIPS:

GFCIs have been required by electrical codes for many years and should be used for receptacle locations along kitchen countertops and in bathrooms, around pools, in some garage areas, and any anywhere near a sink or other water source as well as any damp locations. They can replace any standard receptacle and offer protection from ground-fault hazards on grounded and ungrounded circuits. They do not provide a true ground on ungrounded circuits.

Arc-Fault Circuit-Interrupter (AFCI) Receptacle

DESCRIPTION:

Similar to a GFCI receptacle (page 218), an AFCI works like a standard receptacle but has internal circuitry that senses an arc fault. This might occur when a cord or circuit cable has damaged insulation, allowing electricity to jump across the wires or when a wire comes loose from a connection and the electricity jumps across the gap. Where a GFCI protects you from getting a shock when using the receptacle, an AFCI is like the police of your wiring and helps prevent fires and other hazards that can occur any time. Like GFCIs, AFCI receptacles have TEST and RESET buttons for manually tripping and resetting the internal breaker.

USE:

Standard receptacle use for most areas of the house where a GFCI receptacle is not used. AFCI protection is required by the National Electrical Code (NEC) for pretty much every area in the house except bathrooms, garages, and laundry rooms. In newer homes, the circuits in these areas have AFCI breakers, which protect the entire circuit. If you're replacing old receptacles, it's a good idea to use an AFCI receptacle at that location or to install an AFCI receptacle for the first outlet in the circuit, thereby protecting all the receptacles beyond it in the circuit.

AFCI receptacle (with coverplate).

CHAPTER 32

ELECTRICAL WIRE & CONNECTORS

ABOUT ELECTRICAL WIRE

Terminology for electrical wiring can be confusing to beginners, with good reason. "Wire" is popularly used to refer to anything from a thin metal strand of wire to an appliance cord to a heavy-duty circuit cable. In the trade, *wire* is the metal conductor only, the part that carries the electrical current. It may be solid metal or stranded. If it is covered in plastic insulation, it is called *insulated wire*. In the code books, wires are usually called *conductors*.

Cable is a material made up of a collection of wires inside a protective cover of flexible plastic or metal. Cables may contain two or more insulated or bare-metal wires. Most of the electrical devices in a home are connected to the home's service panel (breaker box) via cable, specifically nonmetallic (NM) cable, rather than individual wires. NM cable is hidden in wall, ceiling, and floor cavities to protect it from damage and keep it out of sight. When wiring is installed in exposed areas, individual wires or cable are often run through rigid metal or plastic *conduit* (see Chapter 34) for protection.

Most wire, or conductors, in household wiring is made of copper. The size of the conductor is specified by a number relating to its gauge, or diameter, followed by "AWG," for American Wire Gauge. Generally speaking, larger conductors have more capacity, meaning they can carry more electrical current without overheating than can smaller conductors. The higher the gauge number, the smaller the wire. Household wiring typically ranges from about 20 AWG at the small end to 6 AWG at the large end. Standard 120-volt circuit cable has 14 AWG wires for 15-amp service or 12 AWG wires for 12-amp service. "AWG" and "gauge" are often used interchangeably.

NOTE:

Always use the proper type and gauge of wire or cable for the circuit it will be installed on.

Low-Voltage Wire

TYPES:

Bell, or doorbell, wire
Thermostat wire
Landscape lighting wire

DESCRIPTION & USE:

Insulated copper wire or cable for use with low-voltage household systems.

BELL:

Typically 20-gauge, with two insulated wires wound together. Rated for up to 30 volts. Used primarily for doorbells but also for some thermostats and low-voltage hobby work.

THERMOSTAT:

Typically 18-gauge. Cable containing five or more insulated wires. Used for thermostats.

LANDSCAPE LIGHTING WIRE:

Cable containing two 12-gauge wires separated by insulation. Looks and feels similar to lamp cord. Rated for outdoor use and ground burial. Voltage ratings may be up to 150 volts, but this cable is intended for low-voltage landscape lighting only; do not use it for other purposes.

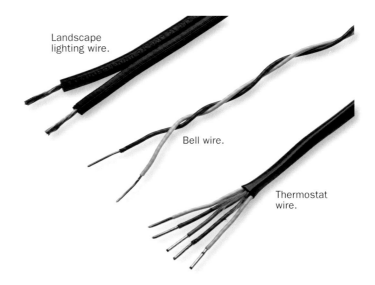

Landscape lighting wire.

Bell wire.

Thermostat wire.

USE TIPS:

Wiring systems for doorbells, thermostats, and landscape lighting are low-voltage only after the *transformer*, a device that steps down the voltage from the standard household current of 120 volts to under 50 volts. The circuit wiring between the supply source and the transformer is standard voltage and calls for standard circuit wiring/cable, not low-voltage wiring.

Telephone Cable

DESCRIPTION:

Low-voltage cable containing four or eight insulated wires. Eight-wire cable, also called "four-pair," has extra wires that are left unattached when connected to conventional phone jacks and plugs. The extras are there for future expansion. Sold in various lengths up to 25 feet with preattached phone-plug ends and in longer rolls without plug ends.

USE:

Connecting conventional telephones and jacks.

Telephone cable.

USE TIPS:

Phone wiring is low-voltage and safe to work on inside your house. To extend an existing phone line or add a new branch line, make the wiring connections following the color coding on existing devices. Your phone company may recommend four- or eight-wire cable for different applications, or you can just match what you already have. For internet connections, Cat 5 cable (page 222) is recommended over phone cable.

Category 5 (Cat 5) Cable

ALSO KNOWN AS:
Data cable.

DESCRIPTION:
Low-voltage cable, similar to phone cable, containing eight insulated wires. Four of the wires are colored, and each is wrapped with a white wire.

Cat 5 cable.

USE:
Used everywhere for information and data networks. In a home, Cat 5 cable is recommended for hard-wired connections to computer modems and other devices for data (internet) service connection. It offers better transmission capacity and fidelity than standard phone cable.

Lamp Cord

ALSO KNOWN AS:
Lamp wire, zip cord.

DESCRIPTION:
Insulated cable or cord containing two 18-gauge wires. Commonly sold in two types: SPT-1 has thinner insulation and is rated for 7 amps; SPT-2 has thicker insulation and is rated for 10 amps.

USE:
Power cords for lamps and other light fixtures. Commonly used for hanging fixtures. Also used for fans and similar low-demand appliances.

USE TIPS:
Cord plugs and line switches (page 216) are designed for either SPT-1 or SPT-2 lamp cord. A switch designed for SPT-1 cord won't fit properly over SPT-2 cord, and vice versa. Always match the cord and switch (or other device) for a safe installation.

NM cable (14/2 top; 12/2 bottom).

Nonmetallic (NM) Cable

ALSO KNOWN AS:

Romex® (brand name).

BX:

Armored metallic cable, armored electrical cable, bushed armored cable, spiral armored cable.

ROMEX®:

Nonmetallic sheathed cable, NM cable, loom wire.

DESCRIPTION:

Flexible cable with two or three insulated copper wires and a bare copper ground wire encased in a vinyl sheathing, often with a wrapping of paper inside. Printing on the sheathing indicates the cable type, the wire gauge, and the number of wires:

14/2 NM-B:

Contains two insulated 14-gauge wires—one with black insulation and one with white—plus a bare ground wire. The ground isn't counted in the numbering system. If the numbers are followed by "G," "W/G," or "w/grd," this simply means "with a ground wire." White sheathing. Rated for 15-amp household circuits. The "B" distinguishes today's NM cable from an older version that has insulation with lower heat-resistance.

14/2 NM-B:

Contains three 14-gauge wires—black, white, and red—plus a ground. White sheathing. Used for 15-amp circuits requiring two "hot" wires (typically the black and red).

12/2 NM-B:

Two 12-gauge wires plus ground. Yellow sheathing. Rated for 20-amp circuits.

12/3 NM-B:

Three 12-gauge wires plus ground. Yellow sheathing. Used for 20-amp circuits requiring two "hot" wires. In addition to standard NM cables, common specialty types include *UF* cable (similar to NM but with gray sheathing; rated for ground burial) and heavy cable with 10-, 8-, or 6-gauge wires, used for 240-volt household circuits and rated for 30, 40, and 55 amps, respectively.

USE:

The standard electrical cabling for interior wiring runs in households. Cable is run through framing cavities and secured to wood framing members with insulated cable staples (page 226). Ends of cables must be secured at each electrical box or fixture with an appropriate cable clamp.

BUYING TIPS:

Sold in precut lengths of 25 and 50 feet and in bulk (by the foot), cut to the length you require. Always buy pieces longer than you need so you don't come up short. It is okay to splice cable lengths together, but this must be done inside a covered electrical box in an accessible location.

Metal Clad (MC) Cable

MC cable

DESCRIPTION:

Flexible metal cable consisting of three or four insulated wires, including an insulated ground wire, wrapped in paper and encased in galvanized-steel, spiral tubing. For standard 120-volt household circuits, the wiring is either 14-gauge (for 15-amp circuits) or 12-gauge (for 20-amp circuits).

USE:

Used in place of NM cable (page 223) when the cable will be exposed and thus needs the added protection of the metal casing.

THHN/THWN Wire

DESCRIPTION:

Individual insulated copper wire with a range of standard colors for identifying wires during installation and when making wiring connections. The wire's names are abbreviations indicating the insulation type

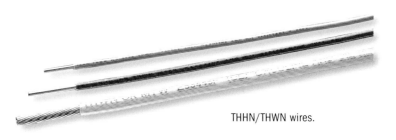

THHN/THWN wires.

and performance ratings: T indicates thermoplastic insulation; H means heat-resistant (two Hs indicate high heat-resistance); W means the wire is suitable for wet locations; N means the wire is impervious to damage from oil and gas. Most common gauges are 14-gauge, for 15-amp circuits; and 12-gauge, for 20-amp circuits. Wires are sold individually, in bulk (by the foot) and long spools up to 500 feet.

USE:

Household wiring runs inside of conduit (see Chapter 34).

Wire Connectors

ALSO KNOWN AS:

Wire-Nut® (brand name), twist-on wire connectors.

Wire connectors.

DESCRIPTION:

Plastic caps with threaded metal inserts for gripping the bare ends of copper wires. Various colors according to size. Size indicates how many and what gauge of wires can be safely secured with the connector. Refer to the manufacturer's instructions, as color-size coding is different among brands. *Push-in wire connectors* are a relatively new variation on classic twist-on types.

USE:

Connects and insulates the bare-metal ends of wires. The standard—and proper—method for connecting wires, as opposed to the old standby, electrical tape, which alone does not create a suitable connection. Used inside electrical boxes, lighting fixtures, and other electrical housings.

USE TIPS:

Many electricians like to twist the bare ends of wires together (using linesman's pliers) before capping them with a wire connector. Alternatively, some wire connector manufacturers may specify inserting the straight ends of wires into the connector, without twisting. With either method, strip the same amount (about ½ to ¾ inch) of insulation from each wire before installing the connector, which should cover all of the bare wire when installed. (This does not apply to bare copper ground wire.)

BUYING TIPS:

Assortment packs of connectors are handy to have around the house because you run into all different wire types, sizes, and quantities with many electrical projects.

Crimp Connectors

DESCRIPTION:

Small metal wire connectors that are crimped (squeezed) onto the ends of light-gauge wires. Color-coded for wire gauge; coloring may vary by manufacturer. Connector end, or *terminal*, may be a ring, a fork-shaped spade terminal, or a slip-on female connector with or without an insulated cover. Installed onto wire ends with a crimping tool.

Crimp connectors.

USE:

Connecting light-gauge wires. Commonly used with small motors and automotive wiring connections. Specific connector sizes must be used with specific wire sizes.

Cable Staples

DESCRIPTION:

Small plastic clips with metal staples or nails. Better types have a molded U-shaped piece with one or more nails; cheaper versions may simply have a plastic strip covering the closed end of a large staple. Available in a range of styles for various cable shapes and sizes, including stackable versions that can hold multiple cables.

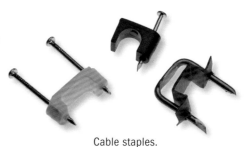

Cable staples.

USE:

Securing insulated electrical cable (typically NM cable; see page 223) or insulated wire to wood framing and other supports.

CHAPTER 33

ELECTRICAL BOXES & CONDUIT

ABOUT ELECTRICAL BOXES

All electrical wiring connections—including connections to receptacles, switches, and fixtures and wire-to-wire connections—must be enclosed inside a noncombustible housing. This is the job of the electrical box (although some fixtures have their own boxes). Boxes anchor the incoming cables via cable clamps, and they provide means for mounting receptacles, switches, light fixtures, and other devices. They also protect combustibles (namely, wood framing and wall finishes) from live wires, in the event a wire comes loose, and they protect people and critters from touching live wiring.

Boxes come in dozens of different shapes and sizes but can generally be broken down into boxes for walls, boxes for ceilings, and outdoor boxes. Standard box materials include plastic (PVC, fiberglass, or thermoset), galvanized steel, and aluminum. Plastic and metal boxes are interchangeable in many cases but not always. In older homes that don't have ground wires in the circuit cables, metal boxes may be part of a grounding system that grounds the devices through the boxes and metal conduit. Installing a plastic box in this case disables the ground protection. Metal boxes also are used where strength is important, such as for hanging ceiling fans and heavy light fixtures.

Metal boxes are made with open holes or holes plugged with easily removed *knockouts* that can be either pried out (if they have little slots for screwdrivers in them) or knocked out with a hammer. Knockouts are removed for installing cable clamps or fittings for conduit. Plastic boxes typically have integrated cable clamps, each consisting of a springy tab that covers a hole, creating a sort of one-way door. The cable is pushed through the hole and the tab grabs it tightly, preventing the cable from being pulled back out. Some metal boxes have internal clamps that are screwed down tight to the cable.

NOTE:

All cables and conduit must be securely clamped to electrical boxes. Never run a cable through a knockout hole without a clamp; if the cable is pulled or moves over time, it can be cut on the edge of the box, creating a serious shock or fire hazard.

Standard Wall Boxes

TYPES:
Single-gang box
Double-gang box (also triple-gang and four-gang)
4-inch square box

DESCRIPTION & USE:
Plastic or metal boxes with a variety of interior capacity. Standard boxes may be called "new work" because they are installed while wall framing is exposed. Many have preattached nails or mounting brackets for installation. Size and shape generally are determined by the number of devices the box will contain:

Triple-gang
plastic box.

Single-gang
plastic box.

Double-gang plastic box
(with mounting bracket).

SINGLE-GANG:

Used for a single switch or receptacle. Comes in three sizes: 18, 20.4, and 22.5 cubic inches. Sometimes called a "gem box."

DOUBLE-, TRIPLE- AND FOUR-GANG:

Used for two, three, or four switches or receptacles, respectively.

4-INCH SQUARE:

Sometimes called a "four-square." Used for one or two switches or receptacles. If one, the box is fitted with an *adapter cover* (page 231) for mounting the device over the center of the box. Some electricians prefer these for single devices because they provide ample room for wiring. In some cases the wall will be too shallow to mount a single-gang box. Here, the shallower four-inch box can be used because it still has the cubic-inch capacity to accommodate the wires. May also be used on the ceiling. Also the most common box type for junctions (wire-to-wire connections); in this case, the box is fitted with a flat metal cover.

BUYING TIPS:

Box size is important. The NEC and most local codes specify the gauge and number of cables that can exit a box of a given size. As a general rule, the device and all wiring should occupy no more than 75 percent of the box interior. Overcrowded boxes can overheat the wiring, and devices and wiring can be damaged when crammed into a box that's too small. When in doubt, use a bigger box.

Ceiling Box

ALSO KNOWN AS:

Fixture box.

DESCRIPTION:

Plastic or metal box in two common shapes: round and octagonal (not a true octagon; more like a square with angled corners). Typically about 4 inches in diameter and 2 ⅛ inches deep. Holes in the back of the box accept screws for mounting directly to wood framing. Alternatively, box may include metal *brace bars* for securing the box between neighboring ceiling joists or rafters (these come in a range of types and strengths). A shallow version of a ceiling box (about 1½ inches deep), known as a "pancake box," is used for surface mounting onto a ceiling for certain fixture types.

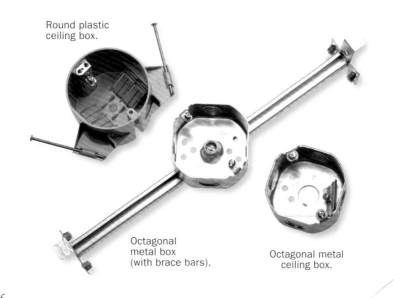

Round plastic ceiling box.

Octagonal metal box (with brace bars).

Octagonal metal ceiling box.

USE:

Mounting overhead and other fixtures and housing wiring connections. Typically installed horizontally (for ceiling fixtures) but can be mounted in a wall for wall-mounted fixtures, such as sconces.

USE TIPS:

Use plastic boxes only for lightweight fixtures. Use metal boxes for heavier light fixtures and always for ceiling fans. Metal boxes are rated for the weight load they can bear. Make sure the box (and any brace bars, if applicable) are more than strong enough for your fan or fixture.

Remodeling Box

ALSO KNOWN AS:
Old work box, cut-in box, retrofit box, remodel box.

DESCRIPTION:
Wall or ceiling boxes with special "ears" or tabs that secure the box to drywall or other wall or ceiling finish. Most commonly plastic but also available in metal. Sold in several standard box types, including single-, double-, triple-, and four-gang wall boxes and ceiling boxes (for lightweight fixtures only).

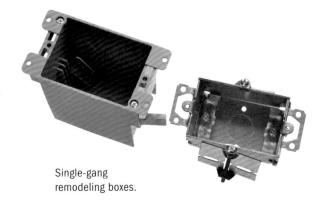

Single-gang remodeling boxes.

USE:
Adding new boxes after the ceiling or wall framing is covered, thus "remodeling." Plastic boxes with ears are inserted into a hole cut into the drywall. When the screws are turned, the ears rotate and are pulled tightly to the backside of the drywall.

Weatherproof Box

ALSO KNOWN AS:
Outdoor box, outside box.

DESCRIPTION:
Heavy-duty rectangular, square, or round box with threaded holes in sides, rear, bottom, and/or top to accept correspondingly threaded conduit fittings or outdoor light fixtures. Includes threaded *closure plugs* for filling unused holes. Commonly aluminum or high-impact PVC. Can be fitted with a gasketed box cover to keep out moisture.

Weatherproof single-gang box.

Weatherproof fixture box (with closure plugs).

USE:
Housing exterior switches and receptacles and for mounting fixtures. Typically surface-mounted to an exterior wall.

Box Covers

DESCRIPTION:

Rigid covers for electrical boxes for indoor or outdoor use. Metal or plastic in a variety of shapes—rectangular, square, octagonal, round—to fit over matching box shapes. May have cutouts for receptacles, switches, and other devices. *Blank* covers have no cutouts and are used for junction boxes. *Weatherproof* (outdoor) box covers have a neoprene gasket to create a watertight seal against the box. An *adapter cover*, also called a mud ring or plaster ring, is installed over a four-inch square box for mounting one or two devices; these have a raised flange around the cutout that matches the thickness of the drywall or other finish material.

Single-gang metal adapter cover.

Blank metal cover for 4" square box.

In-use receptacle cover.

Plastic cover for single toggle switch.

Plastic cover for duplex receptacle.

USE:

Enclosing the front of electrical boxes with or without devices.

USE TIPS:

Today's outdoor/weatherproof receptacle covers are much better than the old-style hinged caps that covered each half of the receptacle and offered no protection when the receptacle was being used. The new standard is the *in-use* or *while-in-use* cover, which has a plastic dome that covers the entire face of the receptacle and any cords that are plugged in. Rounded recesses in the bottom edge of the dome allow the cover to fit over the cords.

Box Extender

ALSO KNOWN AS:

Goof ring.

DESCRIPTION:

Square or rectangular sleeve that slips into an electrical box to effectively extend the sides of the box so it is flush with the wall or ceiling finish. Made of plastic or metal and comes in various sizes for different box designs.

Box extender.

USE:

Extending boxes that are set too deeply and providing solid mounting surface for receptacles, switches, and other devices.

USE TIPS:

Box extenders fix two common problems at once. When boxes are installed too deeply, they create a gap between the box cover and the edge of the box, so that the wall/ceiling finish becomes part of the box interior—a common code violation and fire hazard. This usually also means receptacles and switches aren't mounted securely and are mostly held in place by the box cover screw. Goof rings typically can be installed without rewiring the device.

Cable Clamps

NOT TO BE CONFUSED WITH:

Cable clamps for wire rope/cable (page 63).

Metal cable clamp (with locknut).

DESCRIPTION:

Metal or plastic fitting that slips over the end of NM cable (page 223) and is secured to the cable and a knockout hole in an electrical box. Metal clamps have a separate plate that is screwed tight onto the cable and a threaded end that is secured inside the electrical box with a locknut. Plastic *snap-in*, or *push-in*, connectors clamp onto the cable once they are snapped into the hole in the box.

USE:

Securely connecting NM cable to electrical boxes and fixture housings.

ABOUT CONDUIT

Electrical conduit is metal or plastic tubing used to house and protect wiring in exposed indoor locations, outdoors, and underground. It comes in a few different types, and you are required to use whatever the local electrical code specifies for a given application. Lengths of conduit are joined together and are connected to electrical boxes and fixtures with special fittings designed for the conduit material, size, and application. Conduit runs are secured to supporting structures with pipe straps, which are also specific to the conduit material.

Metal Conduit

TYPES:

Electrical Metallic Tubing (EMT)
Intermediate Metallic Conduit (IMC)
Rigid Metal Conduit (RMC)
Flexible Metal Conduit (FMC)

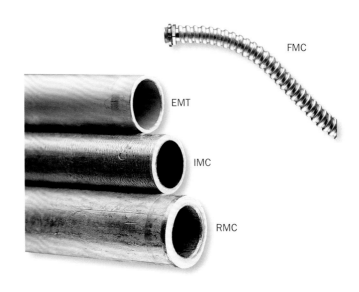

DESCRIPTION & USE:

EMT:

Also known as *thin-wall* conduit. Lightweight rigid steel pipe, typically ½-inch diameter but available up to 4 inches. Most common type of rigid conduit for residential work. Used in basements, garages, outbuildings, and in some exposed outdoor applications. Standard fittings are for interior use only. *Rain-tight* fittings are for damp locations. Not suitable for ground burial.

IMT:

Rigid metal conduit, thicker than EMT but lighter-weight than RMC. For indoor and outdoor applications. Typically used for residential projects only when code does not allow EMT but does not require RMC.

RMC:

Also known as *heavy-wall* conduit. Rigid steel pipe with threaded ends that require threaded fittings. Has thicker wall than IMT (and EMT). Commonly used to protect service entrance cables (electric utility lines) where they anchor to the house and run to the main service panel (breaker box).

FMC:
Also called *greenfield* or "flex." Flexible tubing with spiraled metal construction. Used indoors where rigid metal is difficult to install and/or rigidity is not required or flexibility is desirable (to deal with vibration, for example). Usually seen on hard-wired appliances, such as furnaces, hot water heaters, garbage disposers, and air conditioners. Suitable for dry locations only.

Nonmetallic (Plastic) Conduit

ALSO KNOWN AS:
Rigid Nonmetallic Conduit (RNC), PVC conduit.

Nonmetallic conduit.

DESCRIPTION:
Rigid PVC pipe similar to PVC plumbing pipe but designed specifically for electrical work (do not use PVC plumbing pipe for electrical applications). Has one belled (female) end for receiving straight (male) end of adjacent pipe.

USE:
Indoor and some outdoor applications, including ground burial. Conduit runs are glued together and to fittings with solvent cement (page 152).

USE TIPS:
PVC conduit is less expensive and easier to work with than rigid metal conduit, but it is not always allowed by code; confirm its suitability with the local building department.

Conduit Fittings & Fasteners

DESCRIPTION & USE:
Fittings come in a variety of styles for joining lengths of conduit, turning corners in conduit runs, providing access for pulling wires through conduit, and for connecting conduit to electrical boxes. Fasteners are simple metal or plastic devices for securing conduit to walls, ceilings, and other support structures. They may be U-shaped straps with one or two ears (with holes for screws) or a C-shaped clip with one screw or a circular band with a bolt and nut for tightening over the conduit. Common fittings include:

COUPLING:
Cylinder with two setscrews for joining to lengths conduit.

ELBOW:
Creates a 90° turn, like a plumbing elbow. A *pull elbow* has a cap over the bend that can be removed for pulling and feeding wires through the conduit.

CONDUIT BODY:

Large fitting similar to a pull elbow but with a larger cavity for pulling or splicing wires. Several types, including *LB* (turns 90° with outlet in back), *LL/LR* (90° with outlet to left/right), *C* (two outlets in straight line), and *T* (three outlets, two in straight line, one perpendicular to other two).

RAIN-TIGHT FITTING:

Compression fitting with rubber gaskets for joining conduit pieces or connecting to boxes, creating watertight seal for wet locations.

LB fitting.

Coupling fitting.

Offset connector.

90° pull elbow.

Two-hole conduit strap.

One-hole conduit strap.

Cable Raceway

ALSO KNOWN AS:

Wire channel.

DESCRIPTION:

Metal or plastic channel, typically with a square profile and a finished appearance. Usually includes two pieces: a flat mounting strip that is screwed to the wall or ceiling and a C-shaped channel that snaps onto the mounting strip. Sold with matching fittings for turning corners and splicing channel pieces together. Commonly used with surface-mount electrical boxes.

USE:

Concealing and protecting electrical cords, cables, or wiring on the surface of walls in the place of conduit. Enables house wiring, both permanent and temporary, to be installed without piercing walls. Metal versions are typically for surface-mounted wiring systems (appropriate for adding a receptacle or switch). Plastic versions may be suitable only for temporary wire management, primarily to conceal power cords and phone/data cable.

INDEX